THE OERA LINDA BOOK

ANONYMOUS

ENGLISH TRANSLATION
BY DR. OTTEMA & WILLIAM R. SANDBACH

Copyright © 2021 Martina Martine Digital Media.
www.martinamartine.com

All rights reserved.

ISBN: 9798596177350

Translator's Preface

The work of which I here offer an English translation has excited, among the Dutch and German literary societies, a keen controversy in regard to its authenticity—a controversy not yet brought to a conclusion, some affirming that it contains internal evidence of truth, while others declare it to be a forgery. But even the latter do not insist on its being the work of a modern fabricator. They allow it to be one hundred, or perhaps one hundred and fifty, years old. If they admit that, I do not see why they refuse it a greater antiquity; and as to the improbability of the stories related in it, I refer the reader to the exhaustive inquiry in Dr Ottema's Preface.

Is it more difficult to believe that the early Frisians, being hardy and intrepid marine adventurers, sailed to the Mediterranean, and even proceeded farther, than that the Phœnicians sailed to England for tin, and to the Baltic for amber? or that a clever woman became a lawgiver at Athens, than that a goddess sprang, full grown and armed, from the cleft skull of Jupiter?

There is nothing in the narratives of this book inconsistent with probability, however they may vary from some of our preconceived ideas; but whether it is really what it pretends to be—a very ancient manuscript, or a more modern fiction—it is not the less a most curious and interesting work, and as such I offer it to the British public.

In order to give an idea of the manuscript, I have procured photographs of two of its pages, which are bound with this volume.

I have also followed Dr Ottema's plan of printing the original Frisian opposite to the translation, so that any reader possessing a knowledge of the language may verify the correctness of the translation.

In addition to the Preface which I have translated, Dr Ottema has written two pamphlets on the subject of the Oera Linda Book (1. Historical Notes and Explanations; 2. The Royal Academy and Het Oera Linda Bok), both of which would be very valuable to any one who wished to study the controversy respecting the authenticity of the work, but which I have not thought it necessary to translate for the present publication.

There has also appeared in the "Deventer Courant" a series of twelve letters on the same subject. Though written anonymously, I believe they are from the pen of Professor Vitringa. They have been translated into German by Mr Otto.

The writer evidently entered upon his task of criticism with a feeling of disbelief in the authenticity of the book; but in his last letter he admits that, after a minute examination, he is unable to pronounce a positive conviction either for or against it.

His concluding remarks are to the following effect:—

"If the book is a romance, then I must admit that it has been written with a good object, and by a clever man, because the sentiments expressed in it are of a highly moral tendency; and the facts related, so far as they can be controlled by regular history, are not untruthful; and where they deal with events of which we have no historical records, they do not offend our ideas of possibility or even probability."

Wm. R. Sandbach.

Introduction

C. over de Linden, Chief Superintendent of the Royal Dockyard at the Helder, possesses a very ancient manuscript, which has been inherited and preserved in his family from time immemorial, without any one knowing whence it came or what it contained, owing to both the language and the writing being unknown.

All that was known was that a tradition contained in it had from generation to generation been recommended to careful preservation. It appeared that the tradition rests upon the contents of two letters, with which the manuscript begins, from Hiddo oera Linda, anno 1256, and from Liko oera Linda, anno 803. It came to C. over de Linden by the directions of his grandfather, Den Heer Andries over de Linden, who lived at Enkhuizen, and died there on the 15th of April 1820, aged sixty-one. As the grandson was at that time barely ten years old, the manuscript was taken care of for him by his aunt, Aafje Meylhoff, born Over de Linden, living at Enkhuizen, who in August 1848 delivered it to the present possessor.

Dr E. Verwijs having heard of this, requested permission to examine the manuscript, and immediately recognised it as very ancient Fries. He obtained at the same time permission to make a copy of it for the benefit of the Friesland Society, and was of opinion that it might be of great importance, provided it was not supposititious, and invented for some deceptive object, which he feared. The manuscript being placed in my hands, I also felt very doubtful, though I could not understand what object any one could have in inventing a false composition only to keep it a secret. This doubt remained until I had examined carefully-executed facsimiles of two fragments, and afterwards of the whole manuscript—the first sight of which convinced me of the great age of the document.

Immediately occurred to me Caesar's remark upon the writing of the Gauls and the Helvetians in his "Bello Gallico" (i. 29, and vi. 14), "Graecis utuntur literis," though it appears in v. 48 that they were not entirely Greek letters. Caesar thus points out only a resemblance—and a very true one—as the writing, which does not altogether correspond with any known form of letters, resembles the most, on a cursory view, the Greek writing, such as is found on monuments and the oldest manuscripts, and belongs to the form which is called lapidary. Besides, I formed the opinion afterwards that the writer of the latter part of the book had been a contemporary of Caesar.

The form and the origin of the writing is so minutely and fully described in the first part of the book, as it could not be in any other language. It is very complete, and consists of thirty-four letters, among which are three separate forms of a and u, and two of e, i, y, and o, besides four pairs of double consonants—ng, th, ks, and gs. The ng, which as a nasal sound has no particular mark in any other Western language, is an indivisible conjunction; the th is soft, as in English, and is sometimes replaced by d; the gs is seldom met with—I believe only in the word segse, to say, in modern Fries sidse, pronounced sisze.

The paper, of large quarto size, is made of cotton, not very thick, without water-mark or maker's mark, made upon a frame or wire-web, with not very broad perpendicular lines.

An introductory letter gives the year 1256 as that in which this manuscript was written by Hiddo overa Linda on foreign paper. Consequently it must have come from Spain, where the Arabs brought into the market paper manufactured from cotton.

On this subject, W. Wattenbach writes in his "Das Schriftwesen im Mittelalter" (Leipzig, 1871), s. 93:

"The manufacture of paper from cotton must have been in use among the Chinese from very remote times, and must have become known to the Arabs by the conquest of Samarcand about the year 704. In Damascus this manufacture was an important branch of industry, for which reason it was called Charta Damascena. By the Arabians this art was brought to the Greeks. It is asserted that Greek manuscripts of the tenth century written upon cotton paper exist, and that in the thirteenth century it was much more used than parchment. To distinguish it from Egyptian paper it was called Charta bombicina, gossypina, cuttunea, xylina. A distinction from linen paper was not yet necessary. In the manufacture of the cotton paper raw cotton was originally used. We first find paper from rags mentioned by Petrus Clusiacensis (1122–50).

"The Spaniards and the Italians learned the manufacture of this paper from the Arabians. The most celebrated factories were at Jativa, Valencia, Toledo, besides Fabriano in the March of Ancona."[1]

In Germany the use of this material did not become very extended, whether it came from Italy or Spain. Therefore the further this preparation spread from the East and the adjoining countries, the more necessity there was that linen should take the place of cotton. A document of Kaufbeuren on linen paper of the year 1318 is of very doubtful genuineness. Bodman considers the oldest pure linen paper to be of the year 1324, but up to 1350 much mixed paper was used. All carefully-written manuscripts of great antiquity show by the regularity of their lines that they must have been ruled, even though no traces of the ruled lines can be distinguished. To make the lines they used a thin piece of lead, a ruler, and a pair of compasses to mark the distances.

In old writings the ink is very black or brown; but while there has been more writing since the thirteenth century, the colour of the ink is often grey or yellowish, and sometimes quite pale, showing that it contains iron. All this affords convincing proof that the manuscript before us belongs to the middle of the thirteenth century, written with clear black letters between fine lines carefully traced with lead. The colour of the ink shows decidedly that it does not contain iron. By these evidences the date given, 1256, is satisfactorily proved, and it is impossible to assign any later date. Therefore all suspicion of modern deception vanishes.

The language is very old Fries, still older and purer than the Fries Rjuchtboek or old Fries laws, differing from that both in form and spelling, so that it appears to be an entirely distinct dialect, and shows that the locality of the language must have been (as it was spoken) between the Vlie and the Scheldt.

The style is extremely simple, concise, and unembarrassed, resembling that of ordinary conversation, and free in the choice of the words. The spelling is also simple and easy, so that the reading of it does not involve the least difficulty, and yet with all its regularity, so unrestricted, that each of the separate writers who have worked at the book has his own peculiarities, arising from the changes in pronunciation in a long course of years, which naturally must have happened, as the last part of the work is written five centuries after the first.

As a specimen of antiquity in language and writing, I believe I may venture to say that this book is unique of its kind. The writing suggests an observation which may be of great importance.

The Greeks know and acknowledge that their writing was not their own invention. They attribute the introduction of it to Kadmus, a Phenician. The names of their oldest letters, from Alpha to Tau, agree so exactly with the names of the letters in the Hebrew alphabet, with which the Phenician will have been nearly connected, that we cannot doubt that the Hebrew was the origin of the Phenician. But the form of their letters differs so entirely from that of the Phenician and Hebrew writing, that in that particular no connection can be thought of between them. Whence, then, have the Greeks derived the form of their letters?

From "thet bok thêra Adela folstar" ("The Book of Adela's Followers") we learn that in the time when Kadmus is said to have lived, about sixteen centuries before Christ, a brisk trade existed between the Frisians and the Phenicians, whom they named Kadhemar, or dwellers on the coast.

The name Kadmus comes too near the word Kadhemar for us not to believe that Kadmus simply meant a Phenician.

Further on we learn that about the same time a priestess of the castle in the island of Walcheren, Min-erva, also called Nyhellenia, had settled in Attica at the head of a Frisian colony, and had founded a castle at Athens. Also, from the accounts written on the walls of Waraburch, that the Finns likewise had a writing of their own—a very troublesome and difficult one to read—and that, therefore, the Tyrians and the Greeks had learned the writing of Frya. By this representation the whole thing explains itself, and it becomes clear whence comes the exterior resemblance between the Greek and the old Fries writing, which Caesar also remarked among the Gauls; as likewise in what manner the Greeks acquired and retained the names of the Finn and the forms of the Fries writing.

Equally remarkable are the forms of their figures. We usually call our figures Arabian, although they have not the least resemblance to those used by the Arabs. The Arabians did not bring their ciphers from the East, because the Semitic nations used the whole alphabet in writing numbers. The manner of expressing all numbers by ten signs the Arabs learned in the West, though the form was in some measure corresponding with their writing, and was written from left to right, after the Western fashion. Our ciphers seem here to have sprung from the Fries ciphers (siffar), which form had the same origin as the handwriting, and is derived from the lines of the Juul?

The book as it lies before us consists of two parts, differing widely from each other, and of dates very far apart. The writer of the first part calls herself Adela, wife of Apol, chief man of the Linda country. This is continued by her son Adelbrost, and her daughter Apollonia. The first book, running from page 1 to 88, is written by Adela. The following part, from 88 to 94, is begun by Adelbrost and continued by Apollonia. The second book, running from page 94 to 114, is written by Apollonia. Much later, perhaps two hundred and fifty years, a third book is written, from page 114 to 134, by Frethorik; then follows from page 134 to 143, written by his widow, Wiljow; after that from page 144 to 169 by their son, Konereed; and then from page 169 to 192 by their grandson, Beeden. Pages 193 and 194, with which the last part must have begun, are wanting, therefore the writer is unknown. He may probably have been a son of Beeden.

On page 134, Wiljow makes mention of another writing of Adela. These she names "thet bok thêra sanga (thet boek), thêra tellinga," and "thet Hellênia bok;" and afterwards "tha skrifta fon Adela jeftha Hellênia."

To fix the date we must start from the year 1256 of our era, when Hiddo overa Linda made the copy, in which he says that it was 3449 years after Atland was sunk. This disappearance of the old land (âldland, âtland) was known by the Greeks, for Plato mentions in his "Timaeus," 24, the disappearance of Atlantis, the position of which was only known as somewhere far beyond the Pillars of Hercules. From this writing it appears that it was land stretching far out to the west of Jutland, of which Heligoland and the islands of North Friesland are the last barren remnants. This event, which occasioned a great dispersion of the Frisian race, became the commencement of a chronological reckoning corresponding with 2193 before Christ, and is known by geologists as the Cimbrian flood.

On page 80 begins an account in the year 1602, after the disappearance of Atland, and thus in the year 591 before Christ; and on page 82 is the account of the murder of Frâna, "Eeremoeder," of Texland two years later—that is, in 589. When, therefore, Adela commences her writing with her own coming forward in an assembly of the people thirty years after the murder of the Eeremoeder, that must have been in the year 559 before Christ. In the part written by her daughter Apollonia, we find that fifteen months after the assembly Adela was killed by the Finns in an attack by surprise of Texland. This must accordingly have happened 557 years before Christ. Hence it follows that the first book, written by Adela, was of the year 558 before Christ. The second book, by Apollonia, we may assign to about the year 530 before Christ. The latter part contains the history of the known kings of Friesland, Friso, Adel (Ubbo), and Asega Askar, called Black Adel. Of the third king, Ubbo, nothing is said, or rather that part is lost, as the pages 169 to 188 are missing. Frethorik, the first writer, who appears now, was a contemporary of the occurrences which he relates, namely, the arrival of Friso. He was a friend of Liudgert den Geertman, who, as rear-admiral of the fleet of Wichhirte, the sea-king, had come with Friso in the year 303 before Christ, 1890 years after the disappearance of Atland. He has borrowed most of his information from the log-book of Liudgert.

The last writer gives himself out most clearly as a contemporary of Black Adel or Askar, about the middle of his reign, which Furmerius states to have been from 70 before Christ to 11 after the birth of Christ, the same period as Julius Caesar and Augustus. He therefore wrote in the middle of the last century before Christ, and knew of the conquest of Gaul by the Romans. It is thus evident that there elapsed fully two centuries between the two parts of the work.

Of the Gauls we read on page 84 that they were called the "Missionaries of Sydon." And on page 124 "that the Gauls are Druids." The Gauls, then, were Druids, and the name Galli, used for the whole nation, was really only the name of an order of priesthood brought from the East, just as among the Romans the Galli were priests of Cybele.

The whole contents of the book are in all respects new. That is to say, there is nothing in it that we were acquainted with before. What we here read of Friso, Adel, and Askar differs entirely from what is related by our own chroniclers, or rather presents it in quite another light. For instance, they all relate that Friso came from India, and that thus the Frisians were of

Indian descent; and yet they add that Friso was a German, and belonged to a Persian race which Herodotus called Germans (Γερμάνιοι). According to the statement in this book, Friso did come from India, and with the fleet of Nearchus; but he is not therefore an Indian. He is of Frisian origin, of Frya's people. He belongs, in fact, to a Frisian colony which after the death of Nijhellênia, fifteen and a half centuries before Christ, under the guidance of a priestess Geert, settled in the Punjab, and took the name of Geertmen. The Geertmen were known by only one of the Greek writers, Strabo, who mentions them as Γερμᾶνες, differing totally and entirely from the Βραχμᾶνες in manners, language, and religion. The historians of Alexander's expeditions do not speak of Frisians or Geertmen, though they mention Indoscythians, thereby describing a people who live in India, but whose origin is in the distant, unknown North.

In the accounts of Liudgert no names are given of places where the Frieslanders lived in India. We only know that they first established themselves to the east of the Punjab, and afterwards moved to the west of those rivers. It is mentioned, moreover, as a striking fact, that in the summer the sun at midday was straight above their heads. They therefore lived within the tropics. We find in Ptolemy (see the map of Kiepert), exactly 24° N. on the west side of the Indus, the name Minnagara; and about six degrees east of that, in 22° N., another Minnagara. This name is pure Fries, the same as Walhallagara, Folsgara, and comes from Minna, the name of an Eeremoeder, in whose time the voyages of Teunis and his nephew Inca took place.

The coincidence is too remarkable to be accidental, and not to prove that Minnagara was the headquarters of the Frisian colony. The establishment of the colonists in the Punjab in 1551 before Christ, and their journey thither, we find fully described in Adela's book; and with the mention of one most remarkable circumstance, namely, that the Frisian mariners sailed through the strait which in those times still ran into the Red Sea.

In Strabo, book i. pages 38 and 50, it appears that Eratosthenes was acquainted with the existence of the strait, of which the later geographers make no mention. It existed still in the time of Moses (Exodus xiv. 2), for he encamped at Pi-ha-chiroht, the "mouth of the strait." Moreover, Strabo mentions that Sesostris made an attempt to cut through the isthmus, but that he was not able to accomplish it. That in very remote times the sea really did flow through is proved by the result of the geological investigations on the isthmus made by the Suez Canal Commission, of which M. Renaud presented a report to the Academy of Sciences on the 19th June 1856. In that report, among other things, appears the following: "Une question fort controversée est celle de savoir, si à l'époque où les Hebreux fuyaient de l'Egypte sous la conduite de Moïse, les lacs amers faisaient encore partie de la mer rouge. Cette dernière hypothèse s'accorderait mieux que l'hypothèse contraire avec le texte des livres sacrés, mais alors il faudrait admettre que depuis l'époque de Moïse le seuil de Suez serait sorti des eaux."

With regard to this question, it is certainly of importance to fall in with an account in this Frisian manuscript, from which it seems that in the sixteenth century before Christ the connection between the Bitter Lakes and the Red Sea still existed, and that the strait was still navigable. The manuscript further states that soon after the passage of the Geertmen there was an earthquake; that the land rose so high that all the water ran out, and all the shallows and alluvial lands rose up like a wall. This must have happened after the time of Moses, so that at the date of the Exodus (1564 B.C.) the track between Suez and the Bitter Lakes was still navigable, but could be forded dry-foot at low water.

This point, then, is the commencement of the isthmus, after the forming of which, the northern inlet was certainly soon filled up as far as the Gulf of Pelusium.

The map by Louis Figuier, in the "Année scientifique et industrielle" (première année), Paris, Hachette, 1857, gives a distinct illustration of the formation of this land.

Another statement, which occurs only in Strabo, finds also here a confirmation. Strabo alone of all the Greek writers relates that Nearchus, after he had landed his troops in the Persian Gulf, at the mouth of the Pasitigris, sailed out of the Persian Gulf by Alexander's command, and steered round Arabia through the Arabian Gulf. As the account stands, it is not clear what Nearchus had to do there, and what the object of the further voyage was. If, as Strabo seems to think, it was only for geographical discovery, he need not have taken the whole fleet. One or two ships would have sufficed. We do not read that he returned. Where, then, did he remain with that fleet?

The answer to this question is to be found in the Frisian version of the story. Alexander had bought the ships on the Indus, or had had them built by the descendants of the Frisians who settled there—the Geertmen—and had taken into his service sailors from among them, and at the head of them was Friso. Alexander having accomplished his voyage and the transport of his troops, had no further use for the ships in the Persian Gulf, but wished to employ them in the Mediterranean. He had taken that idea into his head, and it must be carried into effect. He wished to do what no one had done before him. For this purpose Nearchus was to sail up the Red Sea, and on his arrival at Suez was to find 200 elephants, 1000 camels, workmen and materials, timber and ropes, &c., in order to haul the ships by land over the isthmus. This work was carried on and accomplished with so much zeal and energy that after three months' labour the fleet was launched in the Mediterranean. That the fleet really came to the Mediterranean appears in Plutarch's "Life of Alexander;" but he makes Nearchus bring the fleet round Africa, and sail through the Pillars of Hercules.

After the defeat at Actium, Cleopatra, in imitation of this example, tried to take her fleet over the isthmus in order to escape to India, but was prevented by the inhabitants of Arabia Petraea, who burnt her ships. (See Plutarch's "Life of Antony.") When Alexander shortly afterwards died, Friso remained in the service of Antigonus and Demetrius, until, having been grievously insulted by the latter, he resolved to seek out with his sailors their fatherland, Friesland. To India he could not, indeed, return.

Thus these accounts chime in with and clear up each other, and in that way afford a mutual confirmation of the events.

Such simple narratives and surprising results led me to conclude that we had to do here with more than mere Saga and Legends. Since the last twenty years attention has been directed to the remains of the dwellings on piles, first observed in the Swiss lakes, and afterwards in other parts of Europe. (See Dr E. Rückert, "Die Pfahlbauten;" Würzburg, 1869. Dr T. C. Winkler, in the "Volksalmanak," t. N. v. A. 1867.) When they were found, endeavours were made to discover, by the existing fragments of arms, tools, and household articles, by whom and when these dwellings had been inhabited. There are no accounts of them in historical writers, beyond what Herodotus writes in book v. chapter 16, of the "Paeonen." The only trace that has been found is in one of the panels of Trajan's Pillar, in which the destruction of a pile village in Dacia is represented.

Doubly important, therefore, is it to learn from the writing of Apollonia that she, as "Burgtmaagd" (chief of the virgins), about 540 years before Christ, made a journey up the Rhine to Switzerland, and there became acquainted with the Lake Dwellers (Marsaten). She describes their dwellings built upon piles—the people themselves—their manners and customs. She relates that they lived by fishing and hunting, and that they prepared the skins of the animals with the bark of the birch-tree in order to sell the furs to the Rhine boatmen, who brought them into commerce. This account of the pile dwellings in the Swiss lakes can only have been written in the time when these dwellings still existed and were lived in. In the second part of the writing, Konerêd oera Linda relates that Adel, the son of Friso (±250 years before Christ), visited the pile dwellings in Switzerland with his wife Ifkja.

Later than this account there is no mention by any writer whatever of the pile dwellings, and the subject has remained for twenty centuries utterly unknown until 1853, when an extraordinary low state of the water led to the discovery of these dwellings. Therefore no one could have invented this account in the intervening period. Although a great portion of the first part of the work—the book of Adela—belongs to the mythological period before the Trojan war, there is a striking difference between it and the Greek myths. The Myths have no dates, much less any chronology, nor any internal coherence of successive events. The untrammelled fancy develops itself in every poem separately and independently. The mythological stories contradict each other on every point. "Les Mythes ne se tiennent pas," is the only key to the Greek Mythology.

Here, on the contrary, we meet with a regular succession of dates starting from a fixed period—the destruction of Atland, 2193 before Christ. The accounts are natural and simple, often naïve, never contradict each other, and are always consistent with each other in time and place. As, for instance, the arrival and sojourn of Ulysses with the Burgtmaagd Kalip at Walhallagara (Walcheren), which is the most mythical portion of all, is here said to be 1005 years after the disappearance of Atland, which coincides with 1188 years before Christ, and thus agrees very nearly with the time at which the Greeks say the Trojan war took place. The story of Ulysses was not brought here for the first time by the Romans. Tacitus found it already in Lower Germany (see "Germania," cap. 3), and says that at Asciburgium there was an altar on which the names of Ulysses and his father Laërtes were inscribed.

Another remarkable difference consists in this, that the Myths know no origin, do not name either writers or relaters of their stories, and therefore never can bring forward any authority. Whereas in Adela's book, for every statement is given a notice where it was found or whence it was taken. For instance, "This comes from Minno's writings—this is written on the walls of Waraburch—this in the town of Frya—this at Stavia—this at Walhallagara."

There is also this further. Laws, regular legislative enactments, such as are found in great numbers in Adela's book, are utterly unknown in Mythology, and indeed are irreconcilable with its existence. Even when the Myth attributes to Minos the introduction of lawgiving in Crete, it does not give the least account of what the legislation consisted in. Also among the Gods of Mythology there existed no system of laws. The only law was unchangable Destiny and the will of the supreme Zeus.

With regard to Mythology, this writing, which bears no mythical character, is not less remarkable than with regard to history. Notwithstanding the frequent and various relations with Denmark, Sweden, and Norway, we do not find any traces of acquaintance with the Northern or Scandinavian Mythology. Only Wodin appears in the person of Wodan, a chief of the Frisians, who became the son-in-law of one Magy, King of the Finns, and after his death was deified.

The Frisian religion is extremely simple, and pure Monotheism. Wr-alda or Wr-alda's spirit is the only eternal, unchangeable, perfect, and almighty being. Wr-alda has created everything. Out of him proceeds everything—

first the beginning, then time, and afterwards Irtha, the Earth. Irtha bore three daughters—Lyda, Finda, and Frya—the mothers of the three distinct races, black, yellow, and white—Africa, Asia, and Europe. As such, Frya is the mother of Frya's people, the Frieslanders. She is the representative of Wr-alda, and is reverenced accordingly. Frya has established her "Tex," the first law, and has established the religion of the eternal light. The worship consists in the maintenance of a perpetually-burning lamp, foddik, by priestesses, virgins. At the head of the virgins in every town was a Burgtmaagd, and the chief of the Burgtmaagden was the Eeremoeder of the Fryasburgt of Texland. The Eeremoeder governs the whole country. The kings can do nothing, nor can anything happen without her advice and approval. The first Eeremoeder was appointed by Frya herself, and was called Fâsta. In fact, we find here the prototype of the Roman Vestal Virgins.

We are reminded here of Velleda (Welda) and Aurinia in Tacitus ("Germania," 8. Hist., iv. 61, 65; v. 22, 24. "Annals," i. 54), and of Gauna, the successor of Velleda, in Dio Cassius (Fragments, 49). Tacitus speaks of the town of Velleda as "edita turris," page 146. It was the town Mannagarda forda (Munster). In the county of the Marsians he speaks of the temple Tanfane (Tanfanc), so called from the sign of the Juul. (See plate I.) The last of these towns was Fâstaburgt in Ameland, temple Foste, destroyed, according to Occa Scarlensis, in 806.

If we find among the Frisians a belief in a Godhead and ideas of religion entirely different from the Mythology of other nations, we are the more surprised to find in some points the closest connection with the Greek and Roman Mythology, and even with the origin of two deities of the highest rank, Min-erva and Neptune. Min-erva (Athéné) was originally a Burgtmaagd, priestess of Frya, at the town Walhallagara, Middelburg, or Domburg, in Walcheren. And this Min-erva is at the same time the mysterious enigmatical goddess of whose worship scarcely any traces remain beyond the votive stones at Domburg, in Walcheren, Nehallenia, of whom no mythology knows anything more than the name, which etymology has used for all sorts of fantastical derivations.[2]

The other, Neptune, called by the Etrurians Nethunus, the God of the Mediterranean Sea, appears here to have been, when living, a Friesland Viking, or sea-king, whose home was Alderga (Ouddorp, not far from Alkmaar). His name was Teunis, called familiarly by his followers Neef Teunis, or Cousin Teunis, who had chosen the Mediterranean as the destination of his expeditions, and must have been deified by the Tyrians at the time when the Phenician navigators began to extend their voyages so remarkably, sailing to Friesland in order to obtain British tin, northern iron, and amber from the Baltic, about 2000 years before Christ.

Besides these two we meet with a third mythological person—Minos, the lawgiver of Crete, who likewise appears to have been a Friesland sea-king, Minno, born at Lindaoord, between Wieringen and Kreyl, who imparted to the Cretans an "Asagaboek." He is that Minos who, with his brother Rhadamanthus and AEacus, presided as judges over the fates of the ghosts in Hades, and must not be confounded with the later Minos, the contemporary of AEgeus and Theseus, who appears in the Athenian fables.

The reader may perhaps be inclined to laugh at these statements, and apply to me the words that I myself have lately used, fantastic and improbable. Indeed at first I could not believe my own eyes, and yet after further consideration I arrived at the discovery of extraordinary conformities which render the case much less improbable than the birth of Min-erva from the head of Jupiter by a blow from the axe of Hephaestus, for instance.

In the Greek Mythology all the gods and goddesses have a youthful period. Pallas alone has no youth. She is not otherwise known than adult. Min-erva appears in Attica as high priestess from a foreign country, a country unknown to the Greeks. Pallas is a virgin goddess, Min-erva is a Burgtmaagd. The fair, blue-eyed Pallas, differing thus in type from the rest of the gods and goddesses, evidently belonged to Frya's people. The character for wisdom and the emblematical attributes, especially the owl, are the same for both. Pallas gives to the new town her own name, Athènai, which has no meaning in Greek. Min-erva gives to the town built by her the name Athene, which has an important meaning in Fries, namely, that they came there as friends—"Âthen."

Min-erva came to Attica about 1600 years before Christ, the period at which the Grecian Mythology was beginning to be formed. Min-erva landed with the fleet of Jon at the head of a colony in Attica. In later times we find her on the Roman votive stones in Walcheren, under the name of Nehallenia, worshipped as a goddess of navigation; and Pallas is worshipped by the Athenians as the protecting goddess of shipbuilding and navigation.

Time is the carrier who must eternally turn the "Jol" (wheel) and carry the sun along his course through the firmament from winter to winter, thus forming the year, every turn of the wheel being a day. In midwinter the "Jolfeest" is celebrated on Frya's Day. Then cakes are baked in the form of the sun's wheel, because with the Jol Frya formed the letters when she wrote her "Tex." The Jolfeest is therefore also in honour of Frya as inventor of writing.

Just as this Jolfeest has been changed by Christianity into Christmas throughout Denmark and Germany, and into St Nicholas' Day in Holland; so, certainly, our St Nicholas' dolls—the lover and his sweetheart—are a memorial of Frya, and the St Nicholas letters a memorial of Frya's invention of letters formed from the wheel.

I cannot analyse the whole contents of this writing, and must content myself with the remarks that I have made. They will give an idea of the richness and importance of the contents. If some of it is fabulous, even as fabulous it must have an interest for us, since so little of the traditions of our forefathers remains to us.

An internal evidence of the antiquity of these writings may be found in the fact that the name Batavians had not yet been used. The inhabitants of the whole country as far as the Scheldt are Frya's people—Frieslanders. The Batavians are not a separate people. The name Batavi is of Roman origin. The Romans gave it to the inhabitants of the banks of the Waal, which river bears the name Patabus in the "Tabula Pentingeriana." The name Batavi does not appear earlier than Tacitus and Pliny, and is interpolated in Caesar's "Bello Gallico," iv. 10. (See my treatise on the course of the rivers through the countries of the Frisians and Batavians, p. 49, in "De Vrije Fries," 4th vol. 1st part, 1845.)

I will conclude with one more remark regarding the language. Those who have been able to take only a superficial view of the manuscript have been struck by the polish of the language, and its conformity with the present Friesland language and Dutch. In this they seem to find grounds for doubting the antiquity of the manuscript.

But, I ask, is, then, the language of Homer much less polished than that of Plato or Demosthenes? And does not the greatest portion of Homer's vocabulary exist in the Greek of our day?

It is true that language alters with time, and is continually subject to slight variations, owing to which language is found to be different at different epochs. This change in the language in this manuscript accordingly gives ground for important observations to philologists. It is not only that of the eight writers who have successively worked at the book, each is recognisable by slight peculiarities in style, language, and spelling; but more particularly between the two parts of the book, between which an interval of more than two centuries occurs, a striking difference of the language is visible, which shows what a slowly progressive regulation it has undergone in that period of time. As the result of these considerations, I arrive at the conclusion that I cannot find any reason to doubt the authenticity of these writings. They cannot be forgeries. In the first place, the copy of 1256 cannot be. Who could at that time have forged anything of that kind? Certainly no one. Still less any one at an earlier date. At a later date a forgery is equally impossible, for the simple reason that no one was acquainted with the language. Except Grimm, Richthofen, and Hettema, no one can be named sufficiently versed in that branch of philology, or who had studied the language so as to be able to write in it. And if any one could have done so, there would have been no more extensive vocabulary at his service than that which the East Frisian laws afford. Therefore, in the centuries lately elapsed, the preparation of this writing was quite impossible. Whoever doubts this let him begin by showing where, when, by whom, and with what object such a forgery could be committed, and let him show in modern times the fellow of this paper, this writing, and this language.

Moreover, that the manuscript of 1256 is not original, but is a copy, is proved by the numerous faults in the writing, as well as by some explanations of words which already in the time of the copyist had become obsolete and little known, as, for instance, in page 82 (114), "to thêra flête jefta bedrum;" page 151 (204), "bargum jefta tonnum fon tha besta bjar."

A still stronger proof is that between pages 157 and 158 one or more pages are missing, which cannot have been lost out of this manuscript, because the pages 157 and 158 are on the front and the back of the same leaf.

Page 157 finishes thus: "Three months afterwards Adel sent messengers to all the friends that he had gained, and requested them to send him intelligent people in the month of May." When we turn over the leaf, the other side begins, "his wife, he said, who had been Maid of Texland, had got a copy of it."

There is no connection between these two. There is wanting, at least, the arrival of the invited, and an account of what passed at their meeting. It is clear, therefore, that the copyist must have turned over two pages of the original instead of one. There certainly existed then an earlier manuscript, and that was doubtless written by Liko oera Linda in the year 803.

We may thus accept that we possess in this manuscript, of which the first part was composed in the sixth century before our era, the oldest production, after Homer and Hesiod, of European literature, And here we find in our fatherland a very ancient people in possession of development, civilization, industry, navigation, commerce, literature, and pure elevated ideas of religion, whose existence we had never even conjectured. Hitherto we have believed that the historical records of our people reach no farther back than the arrival of Friso the presumptive founder of the Frisians, whereas here we become aware that these records mount up to more than 2000 years before Christ, surpassing the antiquity of Hellas and equalling that of Israel.

Adela

Okke My Son—

You must preserve these books with body and soul. They contain the history of all our people, as well as of our forefathers. Last year I saved them in the flood, as well as you and your mother; but they got wet, and therefore began to perish. In order not to lose them, I copied them on foreign paper.

In case you inherit them, you must copy them likewise, and your children must do so too, so that they may never be lost.

Written at Liuwert, in the three thousand four hundred and forty-ninth year after Atland was submerged—that is, according to the Christian reckoning, the year 1256. Hiddo, surnamed Over de Linda.—Watch.

Beloved successors, for the sake of our dear forefathers, and of our dear liberty, I entreat you a thousand times never let the eye of a monk look on these writings. They are very insinuating, but they destroy in an underhand manner all that relates to us Frisians. In order to gain rich benefices, they conspire with foreign kings, who know that we are their greatest enemies, because we dare to speak to their people of liberty, rights, and the duties of princes. Therefore they seek to destroy all that we derive from our forefathers, and all that is left of our old customs.

Ah, my beloved ones! I have visited their courts! If Wr-alda permits it, and we do not shew ourselves strong to resist, they will altogether exterminate us.

LIKO, surnamed OVER DE LINDA.
Written at Liudwert,
Anno Domini 803.

The Book of Adela's Followers

Thirty years after the day on which the Volksmoeder was murdered by the commander Magy, was a time of great distress. All the states that lie on the other side of the Weser had been wrested from us, and had fallen under the power of Magy, and it looked as if his power was to become supreme over the whole land. To avert this misfortune a general assembly of the people was summoned, which was attended by all the men who stood in good repute with the Maagden (priestesses). Then at the end of three days the whole council was in confusion, and in the same position as when they came together. Thereupon Adela demanded to be heard, and said:—

You all know that I was three years Burgtmaagd. You know also that I was chosen for Volksmoeder, and that I refused to be Volksmoeder because I wished to marry Apol; but what you do not know is, that I have watched everything that has happened, as if I had really been your Volksmoeder. I have constantly travelled about, observing what was going on. By that means I have become acquainted with many things that others do not know. You said yesterday that our relatives on the other side of the Weser were dull and cowardly; but I may tell you that the Magy has not won a single village from them by force of arms; but only by detestable deceit, and still more by the rapacity of their dukes and nobles.

Frya has said we must not admit amongst us any but free people; but what have they done? They have imitated our enemies, and instead of killing their prisoners, or letting them go free, they have despised the counsel of Frya, and have made slaves of them.

Because they have acted thus, Frya cared no longer to watch over them. They robbed others of their freedom, and therefore lost their own.

This is well known to you, but I will tell you how they came to sink so low. The Finn women had children. These grew up with our free children. They played and gamboled together in the fields, and were also together by the hearth.

There they learned with pleasure the loose ways of the Finns, because they were bad and new; and thus they became denationalised in spite of the efforts of their parents. When the children grew up, and saw that the children of the Finns handled no weapons, and scarcely worked, they took a distaste for work, and became proud.

The principal men and their cleverest sons made up to the wanton daughters of the Finns; and their own daughters, led astray by this bad example, allowed themselves to be beguiled by the handsome young Finns in derision of their depraved fathers. When the Magy found this out, he took the handsomest of his Finns and Magyars, and promised them "red cows with golden horns" to let themselves be taken prisoners by our people in order to spread his doctrines. His people did even more. Children disappeared, were taken away to the uplands, and after they had been brought up in his pernicious doctrines, were sent back.

When these pretended prisoners had learned our language, they persuaded the dukes and nobles that they should become subject to the Magy—that then their sons would succeed to them without having to be elected. Those who by their good deeds had gained a piece of land in front of their house, they promised on their side should receive in addition a piece behind; those who had got a piece before and behind, should have a rondeel (complete circuit); and those who had a rondeel should have a whole freehold. If the seniors were true to Frya, then they changed their course, and turned to the degenerate sons. Yesterday there were among you those who would have called the whole people together, to compel the eastern states to return to their duty. According to my humble opinion, they would have made a great mistake. Suppose that there was a very serious epidemic among the cattle, would you run the risk of sending your own healthy cattle among the sick ones? Certainly not. Every one must see that doing that would turn out very badly for the whole of the cattle. Who, then, would be so imprudent as to send their children among a people wholly depraved? If I were to give you any advice, it would be to choose a new Volksmoeder. I know that you are in a difficulty about it, because out of the thirteen Burgtmaagden that we still have remaining, eight are candidates for the dignity; but I should pay no attention to that.

Teuntia, the Burgtmaagd of Medeasblik, who is not a candidate, is a person of knowledge and sound sense, and quite as attached to our people and our customs as all the rest together. I should farther recommend that you should visit all the citadels, and write down all the laws of Frya's Tex, as well as all the histories, and all that is written on the walls, in order that it may not be destroyed with the citadels.

It stands written that every Volksmoeder and every Burgtmaagd shall have assistants and messengers—twenty-one maidens and seven apprentices.

If I might add more, I would recommend that all the respectable girls in the towns should be taught; for I say positively, and time will show it, that if you wish to remain true children of Frya, never to be vanquished by fraud or arms, you must take care to bring up your daughters as true Frya's daughters.

You must teach the children how great our country has been, what great men our forefathers were, how great we still are, if we compare ourselves to others.

You must tell them of the sea-heroes, of their mighty deeds and distant voyages. All these stories must be told by the fireside and in the field, wherever it may be, in times of joy or sorrow; and if you wish to impress it on the brains and the hearts of your sons, you must let it flow through the lips of your wives and your daughters.

Adela's advice was followed.

These are the Grevetmen under whose direction this book is composed:—

Apol, Adela's husband; three times a sea-king; Grevetman of Ostflyland and Lindaoorden. The towns Liudgarda, Lindahem, and Stavia are under his care.

The Saxman Storo, Sytia's husband; Grevetman over the Hoogefennen and Wouden. Nine times he was chosen as duke or heerman (commander). The towns Buda and Manna-garda-forda are under his care.

Abêlo, Jaltia's husband; Grevetman over the Zuiderfly-landen. He was three times heerman. The towns Aken, Liudburg, and Katsburg are under his care.

Enoch, Dywcke's husband; Grevetman over Westflyland and Texel. He was chosen nine times for sea-king. Waraburg, Medeasblik, Forana, and Fryasburg are under his care.

Foppe, Dunroo's husband; Grevetman over the seven islands. He was five times sea-king. The town Walhallagara is under his care.

This was inscribed upon the walls of Fryasburg in Texland, as well as at Stavia and Medeasblik.

It was Frya's day, and seven times seven years had elapsed since Festa was appointed Volksmoeder by the desire of Frya. The citadel of Medeasblik was ready, and a Burgtmaagd was chosen. Festa was about to light her new lamp, and when she had done so in the presence of all the people, Frya called from her watch-star, so that every one could hear it: "Festa, take your style and write the things, that I may not speak." Festa did as she was bid, and thus we became Frya's children, and our earliest history began.

This is our earliest history.

Wr-alda, who alone is eternal and good, made the beginning. Then commenced time. Time wrought all things, even the earth. The earth bore grass, herbs, and trees, all useful and all noxious animals. All that is good and useful she brought forth by day, and all that is bad and injurious by night.

After the twelfth Juulfeest she brought forth three maidens:—

Lyda out of fierce heat.

Finda out of strong heat.

Frya out of moderate heat.

When the last came into existence, Wr-alda breathed his spirit upon her in order that men might be bound to him. As soon as they were full grown they took pleasure and delight in the visions of Wr-alda.

Hatred found its way among them.

They each bore twelve sons and twelve daughters—at every Juul-time a couple. Thence come all mankind.

Lyda was black, with hair curled like a lamb's; her eyes shone like stars, and shot out glances like those of a bird of prey.

Lyda was acute. She could hear a snake glide, and could smell a fish in the water.

Lyda was strong and nimble. She could bend a large tree, yet when she walked she did not bruise a flower-stalk.

Lyda was violent. Her voice was loud, and when she screamed in anger every creature quailed.

Wonderful Lyda! She had no regard for laws; her actions were governed by her passions. To help the weak she would kill the strong, and when she had done it she would weep by their bodies.

Poor Lyda! She turned grey by her mad behaviour, and at last she died heart-broken by the wickedness of her children. Foolish children! They accused each other of their mother's death. They howled and fought like wolves, and while they did this the birds devoured the corpse. Who can refrain from tears at such a recital?

Finda was yellow, and her hair was like the mane of a horse. She could not bend a tree, but where Lyda killed one lion she killed ten.

Finda was seductive. Her voice was sweeter than any bird's. Her eyes were alluring and enticing, but whoever looked upon them became her slave.

Finda was unreasonable. She wrote thousands of laws, but she never obeyed one. She despised the frankness of the good, and gave herself up to flatterers.

That was her misfortune. Her head was too full, but her heart was too vain. She loved nobody but herself, and she wished that all should love her.

False Finda! Honey-sweet were her words, but those who trusted them found sorrow at hand.

Selfish Finda! She wished to rule everybody, and her sons were like her. They made their sisters serve them, and they slew each other for the mastery.

Treacherous Finda! One wrong word would irritate her, and the cruellest deeds did not affect her. If she saw a lizard swallow a spider, she shuddered; but if she saw her children kill a Frisian, her bosom swelled with pleasure.

Unfortunate Finda! She died in the bloom of her age, and the mode of her death is unknown.

Hypocritical children! Her corpse was buried under a costly stone, pompous inscriptions were written on it, and loud lamentations were heard at it, but in private not a tear was shed.

Despicable people! The laws that Finda established were written on golden tables, but the object for which they were made was never attained. The good laws were abolished, and selfishness instituted bad ones in their place. O Finda! then the earth overflowed with blood, and your children were mown down like grass. Yes, Finda! those were the fruits of your vanity. Look down from your watch-star and weep.

Frya was white like the snow at sunrise, and the blue of her eyes vied with the rainbow.

Beautiful Frya! Like the rays of the sun shone the locks of her hair, which were as fine as spiders' webs.

Clever Frya! When she opened her lips the birds ceased to sing and the leaves to quiver.

Powerful Frya! At the glance of her eye the lion lay down at her feet and the adder withheld his poison.

Pure Frya! Her food was honey, and her beverage was dew gathered from the cups of the flowers.

Sensible Frya! The first lesson that she taught her children was self-control, and the second was the love of virtue; and when they were grown she taught them the value of liberty; for she said, "Without liberty all other virtues serve to make you slaves, and to disgrace your origin."

Generous Frya! She never allowed metal to be dug from the earth for her own benefit, but when she did it it was for the general use.

Most happy Frya! Like the starry host in the firmament, her children clustered around her.

Wise Frya! When she had seen her children reach the seventh generation, she summoned them all to Flyland, and there gave them her Tex, saying, "Let this be your guide, and it can never go ill with you."

Exalted Frya! When she had thus spoken the earth shook like the sea of Wr-alda. The ground of Flyland sunk beneath her feet, the air was dimmed by tears, and when they looked for their mother she was already risen to her watching star; then at length thunder burst from the clouds, and the lightning wrote upon the firmament "Watch!"

Far-seeing Frya! The land from which she had risen was now a stream, and except her Tex all that was in it was overwhelmed.

Obedient children! When they came to themselves again, they made this high mound and built this citadel upon it, and on the walls they wrote the Tex, and that every one should be able to find it they called the land about it Texland. Therefore it shall remain as long as the earth shall be the earth.

Frya's Tex

Prosperity awaits the free. At last they shall see me again. Through him only can I recognise as free who is neither a slave to another nor to himself. This is my counsel:—

1. When in dire distress, and when mental and physical energy avail nothing, then have recourse to the spirit of Wr-alda; but do not appeal to him before you have tried all other means, for I tell you beforehand, and time will prove its truth, that those who give way to discouragement sink under their burdens.
2. To Wr-alda's spirit only shall you bend the knee in gratitude—thricefold—for what you have received, for what you do receive, and for the hope of aid in time of need.
3. You have seen how speedily I have come to your assistance. Do likewise to your neighbour, but wait not for his entreaties. The suffering would curse you, my maidens would erase your name from the book, and I would regard you as a stranger.
4. Let not your neighbour express his thanks to you on bended knee, which is only due to Wr-alda's spirit. Envy would assail you, Wisdom would ridicule you, and my maidens would accuse you of

irreverence.
5. Four things are given for your enjoyment—air, water, land, and fire—but Wr-alda is the sole possessor of them. Therefore my counsel to you is, choose upright men who will fairly divide the labour and the fruits, so that no man shall be exempt from work or from the duty of defence.
6. If ever it should happen that one of your people should sell his freedom, he is not of you, he is a bastard. I counsel you to expel him and his mother from the land. Repeat this to your children morning, noon, and night, till they think of it in their dreams.
7. If any man shall deprive another, even his debtor, of his liberty, let him be to you as a vile slave; and I advise you to burn his body and that of his mother in an open place, and bury them fifty feet below the ground, so that no grass shall grow upon them. It would poison your cattle.
8. Meddle not with the people of Lyda, nor of Finda, because Wr-alda would help them, and any injury that you inflicted on them would recoil upon your own heads.
9. If it should happen that they come to you for advice or assistance, then it behoves you to help them; but if they should rob you, then fall upon them with fire and sword.
10. If any of them should seek a daughter of yours to wife, and she is willing, explain to her her folly; but if she will follow her lover, let her go in peace.
11. If your son wishes for a daughter of theirs, do the same as to your daughter; but let not either one or the other ever return among you, for they would introduce foreign morals and customs, and if these were accepted by you, I could no longer watch over you.
12. Upon my servant Fasta I have placed all my hopes. Therefore you must choose her for Eeremoeder. Follow my advice, then she will hereafter remain my servant as well as all the sacred maidens who succeed her. Then shall the lamp which I have lighted for you never be extinguished. Its brightness shall always illuminate your intellect, and you shall always remain as free from foreign domination as your fresh river-water is distinct from the salt sea.

This Has Fasta Spoken

All the regulations which have existed a century, that is, a hundred years, may by the advice of the Eeremoeder, with the consent of the community, be inscribed upon the walls of the citadel, and when inscribed on the walls they become laws, and it is our duty to respect them all. If by force or necessity any regulations should be imposed upon us at variance with our laws and customs, we must submit; but should we be released, we must always return to our own again. That is Frya's will, and must be that of all her children.

Fasta Said—

Anything that any man commences, whatever it may be, on the day appointed for Frya's worship shall eternally fail, for time has proved that she was right; and it is become a law that no man shall, except from absolute necessity, keep that day otherwise than as a joyful feast.

These are the Laws Established for the Government of the Citadels

1. Whenever a citadel is built, the lamp belonging to it must be lighted at the original lamp in Texland, and that can only be done by the mother.
2. Every mother shall appoint her own maidens. She may even choose those who are mothers in other towns.
3. The mother of Texland may appoint her own successor, but should she die without having done so, the election shall take place at a general assembly of the whole nation.
4. The mother of Texland may have twenty-one maidens and seven assistants, so that there may always be seven to attend the lamp day and night. She may have the same number of maidens who are mothers in other towns.
5. If a maiden wishes to marry, she must announce it to the mother, and immediately resign her office, before her passion shall have polluted the light.
6. For the service of the mother and of each of the Burgtmaidens there shall be appointed twenty-one townsmen—seven civilians of mature years, seven warriors of mature years, and seven seamen of mature years.
7. Out of the seven three shall retire every year, and shall not be replaced by members of their own family nearer than the fourth degree.
8. Each may have three hundred young townsmen as defenders.
9. For this service they must study Frya's Tex and the laws. From the sages they must learn wisdom, from the warriors the art of war, and from the sea-kings the skill required for distant voyages.
10. Every year one hundred of the defenders shall return to their homes, and those that may have been wounded shall remain in the

citadels.
11. At the election of the defenders no burgher or Grevetman, or other person of distinction, shall vote, but only the people.
12. The mother at Texland shall have three times seven active messengers, and three times twelve speedy horses. In the other citadels each maiden shall have three messengers and seven horses.
13. Every citadel shall have fifty agriculturists chosen by the people, but only those may be chosen who are not strong enough to go to war or to go to sea.
14. Every citadel must provide for its own sustenance, and must maintain its own defences, and look after its share of the general contributions.
15. If a man is chosen to fill any office and refuses to serve, he can never become a burgher, nor have any vote. And if he is already a burgher, he shall cease to be so.
16. If any man wishes to consult the mother or a Burgtmaid, he must apply to the secretary, who will take him to the Burgtmaster. He will then be examined by a surgeon to see if he is in good health. If he is passed, he shall lay aside his arms, and seven warriors shall present him to the mother.
17. If the affair concerns only one district, he must bring forward not less than three witnesses; but if it affects the whole of Friesland, he must have twenty-one additional witnesses, in order to guard against any deceptions.
18. Under all circumstances the mother must take care that her children, that is, Frya's people, shall remain as temperate as possible. This is her most important duty, and it is the duty of all of us to help her in performing it.
19. If she is called upon to decide any judicial question between a Grevetman and the community, she must incline towards the side of the community in order to maintain peace, and because it is better that one man should suffer than many.
20. If any one comes to the mother for advice, and she is prepared to give it, she must do it immediately. If she does not know what to advise, he must remain waiting seven days; and if she then is unable to advise, he must go away without complaining, for it is better to have no advice at all than bad advice.
21. If a mother shall have given bad advice out of ill will, she must be killed or driven out of the land, deprived of everything.
22. If her Burgtheeren are accomplices, they are to be treated in a similar manner.
23. If her guilt is doubtful or only suspected, it must be considered and debated, if necessary, for twenty-one weeks. If half the votes are

against her, she must be declared innocent. If two-thirds are against her, she must wait a whole year. If the votes are then the same, she must be considered guilty, but may not be put to death.

24. If any of the one-third who have voted for her wish to go away with her, they may depart with all their live and dead stock, and shall not be the less considered, since the majority may be wrong as well as the minority.

Universal Law

1. All free-born men are equal, wherefore they must all have equal rights on sea and land, and on all that Wr-alda has given.
2. Every man may seek the wife of his choice, and every woman may bestow her hand on him whom she loves.
3. When a man takes a wife, a house and yard must be given to him. If there is none, one must be built for him.
4. If he has taken a wife in another village, and wishes to remain, they must give him a house there, and likewise the free use of the common.
5. To every man must be given a piece of land behind his house. No man shall have land in front of his house, still less an enclosure, unless he has performed some public service. In such a case it may be given, and the youngest son may inherit it, but after him it returns to the community.
6. Every village shall possess a common for the general good, and the chief of the village shall take care that it is kept in good order, so that posterity shall find it uninjured.
7. Every village shall have a market-place. All the rest of the land shall be for tillage and forest. No one shall fell trees without the consent of the community, or without the knowledge of the forester; for the forests are general property, and no man can appropriate them.
8. The market charges shall not exceed one-twelfth of the value of the goods either to natives or strangers. The portion taken for the charges shall not be sold before the other goods.
9. All the market receipts must be divided yearly into a hundred parts three days before the Juul-day.
10. The Grevetman and his council shall take twenty parts; the keeper of the market ten, and his assistants five; the Volksmoeder one, the midwife four, the village ten, and the poor and infirm shall have fifty parts.
11. There shall be no usurers in the market. If any should come, it will be the duty of the maidens to make it known through the whole land, in order that such people may not be chosen for any office,

because they are hard-hearted. For the sake of money they would betray everybody—the people, the mother, their nearest relations, and even their own selves.
12. If any man should attempt to sell diseased cattle or damaged goods for sound, the market-keeper shall expel him, and the maidens shall proclaim him through the country.

In early times almost all the Finns lived together in their native land, which was called Aldland, and is now submerged. They were thus far away, and we had no wars. When they were driven hitherwards, and appeared as robbers, then arose the necessity of defending ourselves, and we had armies, kings, and wars.

For all this there were established regulations, and out of the regulations came fixed laws.

Here Follow the Laws which were thus Established

1. Every Frisian must resist the assailants with such weapons as he can procure, invent, and use.
2. When a boy is twelve years old he must devote one day in seven to learning how to use his weapons.
3. As soon as he is perfect in the use of them they are to be given to him, and he is to be admitted as a warrior.
4. After serving as a warrior three years, he may become a citizen, and may have a vote in the election of the headman.
5. When he has been seven years a voter he then may have a vote for the chief or king, and may be himself elected.
6. Every year he must be re-elected.
7. Except the king, all other officials are re-eligible who act according to Frya's laws.
8. No king may be in office more than three years, in order that the office may not be permanent.
9. After an interval of seven years he may be elected again.
10. If the king is killed by the enemy, his nearest relative may be a candidate to succeed him.
11. If he dies a natural death, or if his period of service has expired, he shall not be succeeded by any blood relation nearer than the fourth degree.
12. Those who fight with arms are not men of counsel, therefore no king must bear arms. His wisdom must be his weapon, and the love of his warriors his shield.

These are the Rights of the Mothers and the Kings

1. If war breaks out, the mother sends her messengers to the king, who sends messengers to the Grevetmen to call the citizens to arms.
2. The Grevetmen call all the citizens together and decide how many men shall be sent.
3. All the resolutions must immediately be sent to the mother by messengers and witnesses.
4. The mother considers all the resolutions and decides upon them, and with this the king as well as the people must be satisfied.
5. When in the field, the king consults only his superior officers, but three citizens of the mother must be present, without any voice. These citizens must send daily reports to the mother, that they may be sure nothing is done contrary to the counsels of Frya.
6. If the king wishes to do anything which his council opposes, he may not persist in it.
7. If an enemy appears unexpectedly, then the king's orders must be obeyed.
8. If the king is not present, the next to him takes command, and so on in succession according to rank.
9. If there is no leader present, one must be chosen.
10. If there is no time to choose, any one may come forward who feels himself capable of leading.
11. If a king has conquered a dangerous enemy, his successors may take his name after their own. The king may, if he wishes, choose an open piece of ground for a house and ground; the ground shall be enclosed, and may be so large that there shall be seven hundred steps to the boundary in all directions from the house.
12. His youngest son may inherit this, and that son's youngest son after him; then it shall return to the community.

Here are the Rules Established for the Security of All Frisians

1. Whenever new laws are made or new regulations established, they must be for the common good, and not for individual advantage.
2. Whenever in time of war either ships or houses are destroyed, either by the enemy or as a matter of precaution, a general levy shall be assessed on the people to make it good again, so that no one may neglect the general welfare to preserve his own interest.
3. At the conclusion of a war, if any men are so severely wounded as

to be unable to work, they shall be maintained at the public expense, and shall have the best seats at festivals, in order that the young may learn to honour them.
4. If there are widows and orphans, they shall likewise be maintained at the public expense; and the sons may inscribe the names of their fathers on their shields for the honour of their families.
5. If any who have been taken prisoners should return, they must be kept separate from the camp, because they may have obtained their liberty by making treacherous promises, and thus they may avoid keeping their promises without forfeiting their honour.
6. If any enemies be taken prisoners, they must be sent to the interior of the country, that they may learn our free customs.
7. If they are afterwards set free, it must be done with kindness by the maidens, in order that we may make them comrades and friends, instead of haters and enemies.

From Minno's Writings

If any one should be so wicked as to commit robbery, murder, arson, rape, or any other crime, upon a neighbouring state, and our people wish to inflict punishment, the culprit shall be put to death in the presence of the offended, in order that no war may arise, and the innocent suffer for the guilty. If the offended will spare his life and forego their revenge, it may be permitted. If the culprit should be a king, Grevetman, or other person in authority, we must make good his fault, but he must be punished.

If he bears on his shield the honourable name of his forefathers, his kinsmen shall no longer wear it, in order that every man may look after the conduct of his relatives.

Laws for the Navigators

Navigator is the title of those who make foreign voyages.
1. All Frya's sons have equal rights, and every stalwart youth may offer himself as a navigator to the Olderman, who may not refuse him as long as there is any vacancy.
2. The navigators may choose their own masters.
3. The traders must be chosen and named by the community to which they belong, and the navigators have no voice in their election.
4. If during a voyage it is found that the king is bad or incompetent, another may be put in his place, and on the return home he may make his complaint to the Olderman.

5. If the fleet returns with profits, the sailors may divide one-third among themselves in the following manner: The king twelve portions, the admiral seven, the boatswains each two portions, the captains three, and the rest of the crew each one part; the youngest boys each one-third of a portion, the second boys half a portion each, and the eldest boys two-thirds of a portion each.
6. If any have been disabled, they must be maintained at the public expense, and honoured in the same way as the soldiers.
7. If any have died on the voyage, their nearest relatives inherit their portion.
8. Their widows and orphans must be maintained at the public expense; and if they were killed in a sea-fight, their sons may bear the names of their fathers on their shields.
9. If a topsailman is lost, his heirs shall receive a whole portion.
10. If he was betrothed, his bride may claim seven portions in order to erect a monument to her bridegroom, but then she must remain a widow all her life.
11. If the community is fitting out a fleet, the purveyors must provide the best provisions for the voyage, and for the women and children.
12. If a sailor is worn out and poor, and has no house or patrimony, one must be given him. If he does not wish for a house, his friends may take him home; and the community must bear the expense, unless his friends decline to receive it.

Useful Extracts from the Writings left by Minno

Minno was an ancient sea-king. He was a seer and a philosopher, and he gave laws to the Cretans. He was born at Lindaoord, and after all his wanderings he had the happiness to die at Lindahem.

If our neighbours have a piece of land or water which it would be advantageous for us to possess, it is proper that we should offer to buy it. If they refuse to sell it, we must let them keep it. This is Frya's Tex, and it would be unjust to act contrary to it.

If any of our neighbours quarrel and fight about any matter except land, and they request us to arbitrate, our best course will be to decline; but if they insist upon it, it must be done honourably and justly.

If any one comes and says, I am at war, you must help me; or another comes and says, My son is an infant and incompetent, and I am old, so I wish you to be his guardian, and to take charge of my property until he is of age, it is proper to refuse in order that we may not come into disputes about matters foreign to our free customs.

Whenever a foreign trader comes to the open markets at Wyringen and

Almanland, if he cheats, he must immediately be fined, and it must be published by the maidens throughout the whole country.

If he should come back, no one must deal with him. He must return as he came.

Whenever traders are chosen to go to trading stations, or to sail with the fleets, they must be well known and of good reputation with the maidens.

If, however, a bad man should by chance be chosen and should try to cheat, the others are bound to remove him. If he should have committed a cheat, it must be made good, and the culprit must be banished from the land in order that our name may be everywhere held in honour.

If we should be ill-treated in a foreign market, whether distant or near, we must immediately attack them; for though we desire to be at peace, we must not let our neighbours underrate us or think that we are afraid.

In my youth I often grumbled at the strictness of the laws, but afterwards I learned to thank Frya for her Tex and our forefathers for the laws which they established upon it. Wr-alda or Alvader has given me many years, and I have travelled over many lands and seas, and after all that I have seen, I am convinced that we alone are chosen by Alvader to have laws. Lyda's people can neither make laws nor obey them, they are too stupid and uncivilised. Many are like Finda. They are clever enough, but they are too rapacious, haughty, false, immoral, and bloodthirsty.

The toad blows himself out, but he can only crawl. The frog cries "Work, work;" but he can do nothing but hop and make himself ridiculous. The raven cries "Spare, spare;" but he steals and wastes everything that he gets into his beak.

Finda's people are just like these. They say a great deal about making good laws, and every one wishes to make regulations against misconduct, but does not wish to submit to them himself. Whoever is the most crafty crows over the others, and tries to make them submit to him, till another comes who drives him off his perch.

The word "Eva" is too sacred for common use, therefore men have learned to say "Evin."

"Eva" means that sentiment which is implanted in the breast of every man in order that he may know what is right and what is wrong, and by which he is able to judge his own deeds and those of others; that is, if he has been well and properly brought up. "Eva" has also another meaning; that is, tranquil, smooth, like water that is not stirred by a breath of wind. If the water is disturbed it becomes troubled, uneven, but it always has a tendency to return to its tranquil condition. That is its nature, just as the inclination towards justice and freedom exists in Frya's children. We derive this disposition from the spirit of our father Wr-alda, which speaks strongly in Frya's children, and will eternally remain so. Eternity is another symbol of Wr-alda, who remains always just and unchangeable.

Eternal and unalterable are the signs wisdom and rectitude, which must be sought after by all pious people, and must be possessed by all judges. If, therefore, it is desired to make laws and regulations which shall be permanent, they must be equal for all men. The judges must pronounce their decisions according to these laws. If any crime is committed respecting which no law has been made, a general assembly of the people shall be called, where judgment shall be pronounced in accordance with the inspiration of Wr-alda's spirit. If we act thus, our judgment will never fail to be right.

If instead of doing right, men will commit wrong, there will arise quarrels and differences among people and states. Thence arise civil wars, and everything is thrown into confusion and destroyed; and, O foolish people! while you are injuring each other the spiteful Finda's people with their false priests come and attack your ports, ravish your daughters, corrupt your morals, and at last throw the bonds of slavery over every freeman's neck.

From Minno's Writings

When Nyhalennia, whose real name was Min-erva, was well established, and the Krekalanders loved her as well as our own people did, there came some princes and priests to her citadel and asked Min-erva, where her possessions lay. Hellenia answered, I carry my possessions in my own bosom. What I have inherited is the love of wisdom, justice, and freedom. If I lose these I shall become as the least of your slaves; now I give advice for nothing, but then I should sell it. The gentlemen went away laughing and saying, Your humble servants, wise Hellenia. But they missed their object, for the people took up this name as a name of honour. When they saw that their shot had missed they began to calumniate her, and to say that she had bewitched the people; but our people and the good Krekalanders understood at once that it was calumny. She was once asked, If you are not a witch, what is the use of the eggs that you always carry with you? Min-erva answered, These eggs are the symbols of Frya's counsels, in which our future and that of the whole human race lies concealed. Time will hatch them, and we must watch that no harm happens to them. The priests said, Well answered; but what is the use of the dog on your right hand? Hellenia replied, Does not the shepherd have a sheep-dog to keep his flock together? What the dog is to the shepherd I am in Frya's service. I must watch over Frya's flocks. We understand that very well, said the priests; but tell us what means the owl that always sits upon your head, is that light-shunning animal a sign of your clear vision? No, answered Hellenia; he reminds me that there are people on earth who, like him, have their homes in churches and holes, who go about in the twilight, not, like him, to deliver us from mice and other plagues, but to invent tricks to steal away the knowledge of other people, in order to take advantage of them, to make slaves of them, and to suck their blood like leeches. Another time they came with a whole troop of people, when the plague was in the country, and said: We are all making offerings to the gods that they may take away the plague. Will you not help to turn away their anger, or have you yourself brought the plague into the land with all your arts? No, said Min-erva; I know no gods that do evil, therefore I cannot ask them to do better. I only know one good spirit, that is Wr-alda's; and as he is good he never does evil. Where, then, does evil come from? asked the priests. All the evil comes from you, and from the stupidity of the people who let themselves be deceived by you. If, then, your god is so exceedingly good, why does he not turn away the bad? asked the priests. Hellenia answered: Frya has placed us here, and the carrier, that is, Time, must do the rest. For all calamities there is counsel and remedy to be found, but Wr-alda wills that we should search it out ourselves, in order that we may become strong and wise. If we will not do that, he leaves us to our own devices, in order that we may experience the results of wise or foolish conduct. Then a prince said, I should think it best to submit. Very possibly, answered Hellenia; for then men would be like sheep, and you and the priests would take care of them, shearing them and leading them to the shambles. This is what our god does not desire, he desires that we should help one another, but that all should be free and wise. That is also our desire, and therefore our people choose their princes, counts, councillors, chiefs, and masters among the wisest of the good men, in order that every man shall do his best to be wise and good. Thus doing, we learn ourselves and teach the people that being wise and acting wisely can alone lead to holiness. That seems very good judgment, said the priests; but if you mean that the plague is caused by our stupidity, then Nyhellenia will perhaps be so good as to bestow upon us a little of that new light of which she is so proud. Yes, said Hellenia, but ravens and other birds of prey feed only on dead carrion, whereas the plague feeds not only on carrion but on bad laws and customs and wicked passions. If you wish the plague to depart from you and not return, you must put away your bad passions and become pure within and without. We admit that the advice is good, said the priests, but how shall we induce all the people under our rule to agree to it? Then Hellenia stood up and said: The sparrows follow the sower, and the people their good princes, therefore it becomes you to begin by rendering yourselves pure, so that you may look within and without, and not be ashamed of your own conduct. Now, instead of purifying the people, you have invented foul festivals, in which they have so long revelled that they wallow like swine in the mire to atone for your evil passions. The people began to mock and to jeer, so that she did not dare to pursue the subject; and one would have thought that they would have called all the people together to drive us out of the land; but no, in place of abusing her they went all about from the heathenish Krekaland to the Alps, proclaiming that it had pleased the Almighty God to send his clever daughter Min-erva, surnamed Nyhellenia, over the sea in a cloud to give people good counsel, and that all who listened to her should become rich and happy, and in the end governors of all the kingdoms of the earth. They erected statues to her on all their altars, they announced and sold to the simple people advice that she had never given, and related miracles that she had never performed. They cunningly made themselves masters of our laws and customs, and by craft and subtlety were able to explain and spread them around. They appointed priestesses under their own care, who were apparently under the protection of Festa, our first Eeremoeder, to watch over the holy lamp; but that lamp they lit themselves, and instead of imbuing the priestesses with wisdom, and then sending them to watch the sick and educate the young, they made them stupid and ignorant, and never allowed them to come out. They were employed as advisers, but the advice which seemed to come from them was but the repetition of the behests of the priests. When Nyhellenia died, we wished to choose another mother, and some of us wished to go to Texland to look for her; but the priests, who were all-powerful among their own people, would not permit it, and accused us before the people of being unholy.

From the Writings of Minno

When I came away from Athenia with my followers, we arrived at an island named by my crew Kreta, because of the cries that the inhabitants raised on our arrival. When they really saw that we did not come to make war, they were quiet, so that at last I was able to buy a harbour in exchange for a boat and some iron implements, and a piece of land. When we had been settled there a short time, and they discovered that we had no slaves, they were very much astonished; and when I explained to them that we had laws which made everybody equal, they wished to have the same; but they had hardly established them before the whole land was in confusion.

The priests and the princes declared that we had excited their subjects to rebellion, and the people appealed to us for aid and protection. When the princes saw that they were about to lose their kingdom, they gave freedom to their people, and came to me to establish a code of laws. The people, however, got no freedom, and the princes remained masters, acting according to their own pleasure. When this storm had passed, they began to sow divisions among us. They told my people that I had invoked their assistance to make myself permanent king. Once I found poison in my food. So when a ship from Flyland sailed past, I quietly took my departure. Leaving alone, then, my own adventures, I will conclude this history by saying that we must not have anything to do with Finda's people, wherever it may be, because they are full of false tricks, fully as much to be feared as their sweet wine with deadly poison.

Here ends Minno's writing.

These are the Three Principles on which these Laws are Founded

1. Everybody knows that he requires the necessaries of life, and if he cannot obtain them he does not know how to preserve his life.
2. All men have a natural desire to have children, and if it is not satisfied they are not aware what evil may spring from it.
3. Every man knows that he wishes to live free and undisturbed, and that others wish the same thing.

To secure this, these laws and regulations are made. The people of Finda have also their rules and regulations, but these are not made according to what is just—only for the advantage of priests and princes—therefore their states are full of disputes and murder.

1. If any man falls into a state of destitution, his case must be brought before the count by the maidens, because a high-minded Frisian cannot bear to do that himself.
2. If any man becomes poor because he will not work, he must be sent out of the country, because the cowardly and lazy are troublesome and ill-disposed, therefore they ought to be got rid of.
3. Every young man ought to seek a bride and to be married at five-and-twenty.
4. If a young man is not married at five-and-twenty, he must be driven from his home, and the younger men must avoid him. If then he will not marry, he must be declared dead, and leave the country, so that he may not give offence.
5. If a man is impotent, he must openly declare that no one has anything to fear from him, then he may come or go where he likes.
6. If after that he commits any act of incontinence, then he must flee away; if he does not, he may be given over to the vengeance of those whom he has offended, and no one may aid him.
7. Any one who commits a theft shall restore it threefold. For a second offence he shall be sent to the tin mines. The person robbed may forgive him if he pleases, but for a third offence no one shall protect him.

These Rules are Made for Angry People

1. If a man in a passion or out of ill will breaks another's limb or puts out an eye or a tooth, he must pay whatever the injured man demands. If he cannot pay, he must suffer the same injury as he has done to the other. If he refuses this, he must appeal to the Burgtmaagd in order to be sent to work in the iron or tin mines until he has expiated his crime under the general law.
2. If a man is so wicked as to kill a Frisian, he must forfeit his own life; but if the Burgtmaagd can send him to the tin mines for his life before he is taken, she may do so.
3. If the prisoner can prove by proper witnesses that the death was accidental, he may go free; but if it happens a second time, he must go to the tin mines, in order to avoid any unseemly hatred or vengeance.

These are the Rules Concerning Bastards

1. If any man sets fire to another's house, he is no Frisian, he is a bastard. If he is caught in the act, he must be thrown into the fire; and wherever he may flee, he shall never be secure from the avenging justice.
2. No true Frisian shall speak ill of the faults of his neighbours. If any man injures himself, but does no harm to others, he must be his own judge; but if he becomes so bad that he is dangerous to others, they must bring it before the count. But if instead of going to the count a man accuses another behind his back, he must be put on the pillory in the market-place, and then sent out of the country, but not to the tin mines, because even there a backbiter is to be feared.
3. If any man should prove a traitor and show to our enemies the paths leading to our places of refuge, or creep into them by night, he must be the offspring of Finda; he must be burnt. The sailors must take his mother and all his relations to a desolate island, and there scatter his ashes, in order that no poisonous herbs may spring from them. The maidens must curse his name in all the states, in order that no child may be called by his name, and that his ancestors may repudiate him.

War had come to an end, but famine came in its place. There were three men who each stole a sack of corn from different owners, but they were all caught. The first owner brought his thief to the judge, and the maidens said everywhere that he had done right. The second owner took the corn away from his thief and let him go in peace. The maidens said he has done well. The third owner went to the thief's house, and when he saw what misery was there, he went and brought a waggon-load of necessaries to relieve their distress. Frya's maidens came around him and wrote his deed in the eternal book, and wiped out all his sins. This was reported to the Eeremoeder, and she had it made known over the whole country.

What is Written Hereunder is Inscribed on the Walls of Waraburgt

What appears at the top is the signs of the Juul—that is, the first symbol of Wr-alda, also of the origin or beginning from which Time is derived; this is the Kroder, which must always go round with the Juul. According to this model Frya formed the set hand which she used to write her Tex. When Fasta was Eeremoeder she made a running hand out of it. The Witkoning—that is, the Sea-King Godfried the Old—made separate numbers for the set hand and for the runic hand. It is therefore not too much that we celebrate it once a year. We may be eternally thankful to Wr-alda that he allowed his spirit to exercise such an influence over our forefathers.

In her time Finda also invented a mode of writing, but that was so high-flown and full of flourishes that her descendants have soon lost the meaning of it.

Afterwards they learned our writing—that is, the Finns, the Thyriers, and the Krekalanders—but they did not know that it was taken from the Juul, and most therefore always be written round like the sun. Furthermore, they wished that their writing should be illegible by other people, because they always had matters to conceal. In doing this they acted very unwisely, because their children could only with great difficulty read the writings of their predecessors, whereas our most ancient writings are as easy to read as those that were written yesterday.

Here is a specimen of the set hand and of the running hand, as well as of the figures, in both.

This Stands Inscribed upon All Citadels

Before the bad time came our country was the most beautiful in the world. The sun rose higher, and there was seldom frost. The trees and shrubs produced various fruits, which are now lost. In the fields we had not only barley, oats, and rye, but wheat which shone like gold, and which could be baked in the sun's rays. The years were not counted, for one was as happy as another.

On one side we were bounded by Wr-alda's Sea, on which no one but us might or could sail; on the other side we were hedged in by the broad Twiskland (Tusschenland, Duitschland), through which the Finda people dared not come on account of the thick forests and the wild beasts.

Eastward our boundary went to the extremity of the East Sea, and westward to the Mediterranean Sea; so that besides the small rivers we had twelve large rivers given us by Wr-alda to keep our land moist, and to show our scafaring men the way to his sea.

The banks of these rivers were at one time entirely inhabited by our people, as well as the banks of the Rhine from one end to the other. Opposite Denmark and Jutland we had colonies and a Burgtmaagd. Thence we obtained copper and iron, as well as tar and pitch, and some other necessaries. Opposite to us we had Britain, formerly Westland, with her tin mines.

Britain was the land of the exiles, who with the help of their Burgtmaagd had gone away to save their lives; but in order that they might not come back they were tattooed with a B on the forehead, the banished with a red dye, the other criminals with blue. Moreover, our sailors and merchants had many factories among the distant Krekalanders and in Lydia. In Lydia (Lybia) the people are black. As our country was so great and extensive, we had many different names. Those who were settled to the east of Denmark were called Jutten, because often they did nothing else than look for amber (jutten) on the shore. Those who lived in the islands were called Letten, because they lived an isolated life. All those who lived between Denmark and the Sandval, now the Scheldt, were called Stuurlieden (pilots), Zeekampers (naval men), and Angelaren (fishermen). The Angelaren were men who fished in the sea, and were so named because they used lines and hooks instead of nets. From there to the nearest part of Krekaland the inhabitants were called Kadhemers, because they never went to sea but remained ashore.

Those who were settled in the higher marches bounded by Twisklanden (Germany) were called Saxmannen, because they were always armed against the wild beasts and the savage Britons. Besides these we had the names Landzaten (natives of the land), Marzaten (natives of the fens), and Woud or Hout zaten (natives of the woods).

How the Bad Time Came

During the whole summer the sun had been hid behind the clouds, as if unwilling to look upon the earth. There was perpetual calm, and the damp mist hung like a wet sail over the houses and the marshes. The air was heavy and oppressive, and in men's hearts was neither joy nor cheerfulness.

In the midst of this stillness the earth began to tremble as if she was dying. The mountains opened to vomit forth fire and flames. Some sank into the bosom of the earth, and in other places mountains rose out of the plain. Aldland, called by the seafaring people, Atland, disappeared, and the wild waves rose so high over hill and dale that everything was buried in the sea. Many people were swallowed up by the earth, and others who had escaped the fire perished in the water.

It was not only in Finda's land that the earth vomited fire, but also in Twiskland (Germany). Whole forests were burned one after the other, and when the wind blew from that quarter our land was covered with ashes. Rivers changed their course, and at their mouths new islands were formed of sand and drift.

During three years this continued, but at length it ceased, and forests became visible. Many countries were submerged, and in other places land rose above the sea, and the wood was destroyed through the half of Twiskland (Germany). Troops of Finda's people came and settled in the empty places. Our dispersed people were exterminated or made slaves. Then watchfulness was doubly impressed upon us, and time taught us that union is force.

This is Inscribed on the Waraburgt by the Aldegamude

The Waraburgt is not a maiden's city, but the place where all the foreign articles brought by sailors were stored. It lies three hours south from Medeasblik.

Thus is the Preface.

Hills, bow your heads; weep, ye streams and clouds. Yes. Schoonland (Scandinavia) blushes, an enslaved people tramples on your garment, O Frya.

This is the History.

One hundred and one years after the submersion of Aldland a people came out of the East. That people was driven by another. Behind us, in Twiskland (Germany), they fell into disputes, divided into two parties, and each went its own way. Of the one no account has come to us, but the other came in the back of our Schoonland, which was thinly inhabited, particularly the upper part. Therefore they were able to take possession of it without contest, and as they did no other harm, we would not make war about it. Now that we have learned to know them, we will describe their customs, and after that how matters went between us. They were not wild people, like most of Finda's race; but, like the Egyptians, they have priests and also statues in their churches. The priests are the only rulers; they call themselves Magyars, and their headman Magy. He is high priest and king in one. The rest of the people are of no account, and in subjection to them. This people have not even a name; but we call them Finns, because although all the festivals are melancholy and bloody, they are so formal that we are inferior to them in that respect. But still they are not to be envied, because they are slaves to their priests, and still more to their creeds. They believe that evil spirits abound everywhere, and enter into men and beasts, but of Wr-alda's spirit they know nothing. They have weapons of stone, the Magyars of copper. The Magyars affirm that they can exorcise and recall the evil spirits, and this frightens the people, so that you never see a cheerful face. When they were well established, the Magyars sought our friendship, they praised our language and customs, our cattle and iron weapons, which they would willingly have exchanged for their gold and silver ornaments, and they always kept their people within their own boundaries, and that outwitted our watchfulness.

Eighty years afterwards, just at the time of the Juulfeest, they overran our country like a snowstorm driven by the wind. All who could not flee away were killed. Frya was appealed to, but the Schoonlanders (Scandinavians) had neglected her advice. Then all the forces were assembled, and three hours from Godasburgt they were withstood, but war continued. Kat or Katerine was the name of the priestess who was Burgtmaagd of Godasburgt. Kat was proud and haughty, and would neither seek counsel nor aid from the mother; but when the Burgtheeren (citizens) knew this, they themselves sent messengers to Texland to the Eeremoeder. Minna—this was the name of the mother—summoned all the sailors and the young men from Oostflyland and Denmark. From this expedition the history of Wodin sprang, which is inscribed on the citadels, and is here copied. At Aldergamude there lived an old sea-king whose name was Sterik, and whose deeds were famous. This old fellow had three nephews. Wodin, the eldest, lived at Lumkamakia, near the Eemude, in Oostflyland, with his parents. He had once commanded troops. Teunis and Inka were naval warriors, and were just then staying with their father at Aldergamude. When the young warriors had assembled together, they chose Wodin to be their leader or king, and the naval force chose Teunis for their sea-king and Inka for their admiral. The navy then sailed to Denmark, where they took on board Wodin and his valiant host.

The wind was fair, so they arrived immediately in Schoonland. When the northern brothers met together, Wodin divided his powerful army into three bodies. Frya was their war-cry, and they drove back the Finns and Magyars like children. When the Magy heard how his forces had been utterly defeated, he sent messengers with truncheon and crown, who said to Wodin: O almighty king, we are guilty, but all that we have done was done from necessity. You think that we attacked your brothers out of ill will, but we were driven out by our enemies, who are still at our heels. We have often asked your Burgtmaagd for help, but she took no notice of us. The Magy says that if we kill half our numbers in fighting with each other, then the wild shepherds will come and kill all the rest. The Magy possesses great riches, but he has seen that Frya is much more powerful than all our spirits together. He will lay down his head in her lap. You are the most warlike king on the earth, and your people are of iron. Become our king, and we will all be your slaves. What glory it would be for you if you could drive back the savages! Our trumpets would resound with your praises, and the fame of your deeds would precede you everywhere. Wodin was strong, fierce, and warlike, but he was not clear-sighted, therefore he was taken in their toils, and crowned by the Magy.

Very many of the sailors and soldiers to whom this proceeding was displeasing went away secretly, taking Kat with them. But Kat, who did not wish to appear before either the mother or the general assembly, jumped overboard. Then a storm arose and drove the ships upon the banks of Denmark, with the total destruction of their crews. This strait was afterwards called the Kattegat. When Wodin was crowned, he attacked the savages, who were all horsemen, and fell upon Wodin's troops like a hailstorm; but like a whirl-wind they were turned back, and did not dare to appear again. When Wodin returned, Magy gave him his daughter to wife. Whereupon he was incensed with herbs; but they were magic herbs, and by degrees he became so audacious that he dared to disavow and ridicule the spirits of Frya and Wr-alda, while he bent his free head before the false and deceitful images. His reign lasted seven years, and then he disappeared. The Magy said that he was taken up by their gods and still reigned over us, but our people laughed at what they said. When Wodin had disappeared some time, disputes arose. We wished to choose another king, but the Magy would not permit it. He asserted that it was his right given him by his idols. But besides this dispute there was one between the Magyars and Finns, who would honour neither Frya nor Wodin; but the Magy did just as he pleased, because his daughter had a son by Wodin, and he would have it that this son was of high descent. While all were disputing and quarrelling, he crowned the boy as king, and set up himself as guardian and counsellor. Those who cared more for themselves than for justice let him work his own way, but the good men took their departure. Many Magyars fled back with their troops, and the sea-people took ship, accompanied by a body of stalwart Finns as rowers.

Next comes upon the stage the history of Neef Teunis and Neef Inka.

All this is Inscribed not only on the Waraburgt, but also on the Burgt Stavia, which Lies Behind the Port of Stavre

When Teunis wished to return home, he went first towards Denmark; but he might not land there, for so the mother had ordered, nor was he to land at Flyland nor anywhere about there. In this way he would have lost all his people by want and hardship, so he landed at night to steal and sailed on by day. Thus coasting along, he at length arrived at the colony of Kadik (Cadiz), so called because it was built with a stone quay. Here they bought all kinds of stores, but Tuntia the Burgtmaagd would not allow them to settle there. When they were ready they began to disagree. Teunis wished to sail through the straits to the Mediterranean Sea, and enter the service of the rich Egyptian king, as he had done before, but Inka said he had had enough of all those Finda's people. Inka thought that perchance some highlying part of Atland might remain as an island, where he and his people might live in peace. As the two cousins could not agree, Teunis planted a red flag on the shore, and Inka a blue flag. Every man could choose which he pleased, and to their astonishment the greater part of the Finns and Magyars followed Inka, who had objected to serve the kings of Finda's people. When they had counted the people and divided the ships accordingly, the fleet separated. We shall hear of Teunis afterwards, but nothing more of Inka.

Neef Teunis coasted through the straits to the Mediterranean Sea. When Atland was submerged there was much suffering also on the shores of the Mediterranean, on which account many of Finda's people, Krekalanders, and people from Lyda's land, came to us. On the other hand, many of our people went to Lyda's land. The result of all this was that the Krekalanders far and wide were lost to the superintendence of the mother. Teunis had reckoned on this, and had therefore wished to find there a good haven from which he might go and serve under the rich princes; but as his fleet and his people had such a shattered appearance, the inhabitants on the coasts thought that they were pirates, and drove them away. At last they arrived at the Phœnician coast, one hundred and ninety-three years after Atland was submerged. Near the coast they found an island with two deep bays, so that there appeared to be three islands. In the middle one they established themselves, and afterwards built a city wall round the place. Then they wanted to give it a name, but disagreed about it. Some wanted to call it Fryasburgt, others Neeftunia; but the Magyars and Finns begged that it might be called Thyrhisburgt.

Thyr was the name of one of their idols, and it was upon his feast-day that they had landed there; and in return they offered to recognise Teunis as their perpetual king. Teunis let himself be persuaded, and the others would not make any quarrel about it. When they were well established, they sent some old seamen and Magyars on an expedition as far as the town of Sidon; but at first the inhabitants of the coast would have nothing to do with them, saying, You are only foreign adventurers whom we do not respect. But when we sold them some of our iron weapons, everything went well. They also wished to buy our amber, and their inquiries about it were incessant. But Teunis, who was far-seeing, pretended that he had no more iron weapons or amber. Then merchants came and begged him to let them have twenty vessels, which they would freight with the finest goods, and they would provide as many people to row as he would require. Twelve ships were then laden with wine, honey, tanned leather, and saddles and bridles mounted in gold, such as had never been seen before.

Teunis sailed to the Flymeer with all this treasure, which so enchanted the Grevetman of Westflyland that he induced Teunis to build a warehouse at the mouth of the Flymeer. Afterwards this place was called Almanaland, and the market where they traded at Wyringen was called Toelaatmarkt. The mother advised that they should sell everything except iron weapons, but no attention was paid to what she said. As the Thyriers had thus free play, they came from far and near to take away our goods, to the loss of our seafaring people. Therefore it was resolved in a general assembly to allow only seven Thyrian ships and no more in a year.

What the Consequence of This Was

In the northernmost part of the Mediterranean there lies an island close to the coast. They now came and asked to buy that, on which a general council was held.

The mother's advice was asked, and she wished to see them at some distance, so she saw no harm in it; but as we afterwards saw what a mistake we had made, we called the island Missellia (Marseilles). Hereafter will be seen what reason we had. The Golen, as the missionary priests of Sidon were called, had observed that the land there was thinly peopled, and was far from the mother. In order to make a favourable impression, they had themselves called in our language followers of the truth; but they had better have been called abstainers from the truth, or, in short, "Triuwenden," as our seafaring people afterwards called them. When they were well established, their merchants exchanged their beautiful copper weapons and all sorts of jewels for our iron weapons and hides of wild beasts, which were abundant in our southern countries; but the Golen celebrated all sorts of vile and monstrous festivals, which the inhabitants of the coast promoted with their wanton women and sweet poisonous wine. If any of our people had so conducted himself that his life was in danger, the Golen afforded him a refuge, and sent him to Phonisia, that is, Palmland. When he was settled there, they made him write to his family, friends, and connections that the country was so good and the people so happy that no one could form any idea of it. In Britain there were plenty of men, but few women. When the Golen knew this, they carried off girls everywhere and gave them to the Britons for nothing. So all these girls served their purpose to steal children from Wr-alda in order to give them to false gods.

Now We Will Write about the War between the Burgtmaagden Kalta and Min-erva

And how we thereby lost all our southern lands and Britain to the Golen. Near the southern mouth of the Rhine and the Scheldt there are seven islands, named after Frya's seven virgins of the week. In the middle of one island is the city of Walhallagara (Middelburg), and on the walls of this city the following history is inscribed. Above it are the words "Read, learn, and watch."

Five hundred and sixty-three years after the submersion of Atland—that is, 1600 years before Christ—a wise town priestess presided here, whose name was Min-erva—called by the sailors Nyhellenia. This name was well chosen, for her counsels were new and clear above all others.

On the other side of the Scheldt, at Flyburgt, Sijrhed presided. This maiden was full of tricks. Her face was beautiful, and her tongue was nimble; but the advice that she gave was always conveyed in mysterious terms. Therefore the mariners called her Kalta, and the landsmen thought it was a title. In the last will of the dead mother, Rosamond was named first, Min-erva second, and Sijrhed third in succession. Min-erva did not mind that, but Sijrhed was very much offended. Like a foreign princess, she wished to be honoured, feared, and worshipped; but Min-erva only desired to be loved. At last all the sailors, even from Denmark and Flymeer, did homage to her. This hurt Sijrhed, because she wanted to excel Min-erva. In order to give an impression of her great watchfulness, she had a cock put on her banner. So then Min-erva went and put a sheep-dog and an owl on her banner. The dog, she said, guards his master and his flock, and the owl watches that the mice shall not devastate the fields; but the cock in his lewdness and his pride is only fit to murder his nearest relations. When Kalta found that her scheme had failed she was still more vexed, so she secretly sent for the Magyars to teach her conjuring. When she had had enough of this she threw herself into the hands of the Gauls; but all her malpractices did not improve her position. When she saw that the sailors kept more and more aloof from her, she tried to win them back by fear. At the full moon, when the sea was stormy, she ran over the wild waves, calling to the sailors that they would all be lost if they did not worship her. Then she blinded their eyes, so that they mistook land for water and water for land, and in this way many a good ship was totally lost. At the first war-feast, when all her countrymen were armed, she brought casks of beer, which she had drugged. When they were all drunk she mounted her war-horse, leaning her head upon her spear. Sunrise could not be more beautiful. When she saw that the eyes of all were fixed upon her, she opened her lips and said:—

Sons and daughters of Frya, you know that in these last times we have suffered much loss and misery because the sailors no longer come to buy our paper, but you do not know what the reason of it is. I have long kept silence about it, but can do so no longer. Listen, then, my friends, that you may know on which side to show your teeth. On the other side of the Scheldt, where from time to time there come ships from all parts, they make now paper from pumpkin leaves, by which they save flax and outdo us. Now, as the making of paper was always our principal industry, the mother willed that people should learn it from us; but Min-erva has bewitched all the people—yes, bewitched, my friends—as well as all our cattle that died lately. I must come out with it. If I were not Burgtmaagd, I should know what to do. I should burn the witch in her nest.

As soon as she had uttered these words she sped away to her citadel; but the drunken people were so excited that they did not stop to weigh what they had heard. In mad haste they hurried over the Sandfal, and as night came on they burst into the citadel. However, Kalta again missed her aim; for Minerva, her maidens, and her lamp were all saved by the alertness of the seamen.

We Now Come to the History of Jon

Jon, Jôn, Jhon, Jan, are all the same name, though the pronuncation varies, as the seamen like to shorten everything to be able to make it easier to call. Jon—that is, "Given"—was a sea-king, born at Alberga, who sailed from the Flymeer with a fleet of 127 ships fitted out for a long voyage, and laden with amber, tin, copper, cloth, linen, felt, otter-skins, beaver and rabbit skins. He would also have taken paper from here, but when he saw how Kalta had destroyed the citadel he became so angry that he went off with all his people to Flyburgt, and out of revenge set fire to it. His admiral and some of his people saved the lamp and the maidens, but they could not catch Sijrhed (or Kalta). She climbed up on the furthest battlement, and they thought she must be killed in the flames; but what happened? While all her people stood transfixed with horror, she appeared upon her steed more beautiful than ever, calling to them, "To Kalta!" Then the other Schelda people poured out towards her. When the seamen saw that, they shouted,

"We are for Min-erva!" from which arose a war in which thousands were killed.

At this time Rosamond the mother, who had done all in her power by gentle means to preserve peace, when she saw how bad it was, made short work of it. Immediately she sent messengers throughout all the districts to call a general levy, which brought together all the defenders of the country. The landsmen who were fighting were all caught, but Jon with his seamen took refuge on board his fleet, taking with him the two lamps, as well as Min-erva and the maidens of both the citadels. Helprik, the chief, summoned him to appear; but while all the soldiers were on the other side of the Scheldt, Jon sailed back to the Flymeer, and then straight to our islands. His fighting men and many of our people took women and children on board, and when Jon saw that he and his people would be punished for their misdeeds, he secretly took his departure. He did well, for all our islanders, and the other Scheldt people who had been fighting were transported to Britain. This step was a mistake, for now came the beginning of the end. Kalta, who, people said, could go as easily on the water as on the land, went to the mainland and on to Missellia (Marseilles). Then came the Gauls out of the Mediterranean Sea with their ships to Cadiz, and along all our coasts, and fell upon Britain; but they could not make any good footing there, because the government was powerful and the exiles were still Frisians. But now came Kalta and said: You were born free, and for small offences have been sent away, not for your own improvement, but to get tin by your labour. If you wish to be free again, and take my advice, and live under my care, come away. I will provide you with arms, and will watch over you. The news flew through the land like lightning, and before the carrier's wheel had made one revolution she was mistress of all the Thyriers in all our southern states as far as the Seine. She built herself a citadel on the high land to the north, and called it Kaltasburgh. It still exists under the name of Kêrenak. From this castle she ruled as a true mother, against their will, not for her followers, but over them, who were thenceforth called Kelts. The Gauls gradually obtained dominion over the whole of Britain, partly because they no longer had any citadel; secondly, because they had there no Burgtmaagden; and thirdly, because they had no real lamps. From all these causes the people could not learn anything. They were stupid and foolish, and having allowed the Gauls to rob them of their arms, they were led about like a bull with a ring in his nose.

Now We Shall Write how it Fared with Jon

It is Inscribed at Texland. Ten years after Jon went away, there arrived three ships in the Flymeer; the people cried Huzza! (What a blessing!) and from their accounts the mother had this written.

When Jon reached the Mediterranean Sea, the reports of the Gauls had preceded him, so that on the nearest Italian coast he was nowhere safe. Therefore he went with his fleet straight over to Lybia. There the black men wanted to catch them and eat them. At last they came to Tyre, but Min-erva said, Keep clear, for here the air has been long poisoned by the priests. The king was a descendant of Teunis, as we were afterwards informed; but as the priests wished to have a king, who, according to their ideas, was of long descent, they deified Teunis, to the vexation of his followers. After they had passed Tyre, the Tyrians seized one of the rearmost ships, and as the ship was too far behind us, we could not take it back again; but Jon swore to be revenged for it. When night came, Jon bent his course towards the distant Krekalanden. At last they arrived at a country that looked very barren, but they found a harbour there. Here, said Min-erva, we need not perhaps have any fear of princes or priests, as they always look out for rich fat lands. When they entered the harbour, there was not room for all the ships, and yet most of the people were too cowardly to go any further. Then Jon, who wished to get away, went with his spear and banner, calling to the young people, to know who would volunteer to share his adventures. Min-erva did the same thing, but she wished to remain there. The greater part stopped with Min-erva, but the young sailors went with Jon. Jon took the lamp of Kalta and her maidens with him. Min-erva retained her lamp and her own maidens.

Between the near and the distant coasts of Italy Jon found some islands, which he thought desirable. Upon the largest he built a city in the wood between the mountains. From the smaller islands he made expeditions for vengeance on the Tyrians, and plundered their ships and their lands. Therefore these islands were called Insulae Piratarum, as well as Johannis Insulae.

When Min-erva had examined the country which is called by the inhabitants Attica, she saw that the people were all goatherds, and that they lived on meat, wild roots, herbs, and honey. They were clothed in skins, and had their dwellings on the slopes (hellinga) of the hills, wherefore they were called Hellingers. At first they ran away, but when they found that we did not attack them, they came back and showed great friendship. Min-erva asked if we might settle there peaceably. This was agreed to on the condition that we should help them to fight against their neighbours, who came continually to carry away their children and to rob their dwellings. Then we built a citadel at an hour's distance from the harbour. By the advice of Min-erva it was called Athens, because, she said, those who come after us ought to know that we are not here by cunning or violence, but were received as friends (âtha). While we were building the citadel the principal personages came to see us, and when they saw that we had no slaves it did not please them, and they gave her to understand it, as they thought that she was a princess. But Min-erva said, How did you get your slaves? They answered, We bought some and took others in war. Min-erva replied, If nobody would buy slaves they would not steal your children, and you would have no wars about it. If you wish to remain our allies, you will free your slaves. The chiefs did not like this, and wanted to drive us away; but the most enlightened of the people came and helped us to build our citadel, which was built of stone.

This is the history of Jon and of Min-erva.

When they had finished their story they asked respectfully for iron weapons; for, said they, our foes are powerful, but if we have good arms we can withstand them. When this had been agreed to, the people asked if Frya's customs would flourish in Athens and in other parts of Greece (Krekalanden). The mother answered, If the distant Greeks belong to the direct descent of Frya, then they will flourish; but if they do not descend from Frya, then there will be a long contention about it, because the carrier must make five thousand revolutions of his Juul before Finda's people will be ripe for liberty.

This is about the Geertmen

When Hellenia or Min-erva died, the priests pretended to be with us, and in order to make it appear so, they deified Hellenia. They refused to have any other mother chosen, saying that they feared there was no one among her maidens whom they could trust as they had trusted Min-erva, surnamed Nyhellenia.

But we would not recognise Min-erva as a goddess, because she herself had told us that no one could be perfectly good except the spirit of Wr-alda. Therefore we chose Geert Pyre's daughter for our mother. When the priests saw that they could not fry their herrings on our fire (have everything their own way), they left Athens, and said that we refused to acknowledge Min-erva as a goddess out of envy, because she had shown so much affection to the natives. Thereupon they gave the people statues of her, declaring that they might ask of them whatever they liked, as long as they were obedient to her. By these kinds of tales the stupid people were estranged from us, and at last they attacked us; but as we had built our stone city wall with two horns down to the sea, they could not get at us. Then, lo and behold! an Egyptian high priest, bright of eye, clear of brain, and enlightened of mind, whose name was Cecrops, came to give them advice.

When he saw that with his people he could not storm our wall, he sent messengers to Tyre. Thereupon there arrived three hundred ships full of wild mountain soldiers, which sailed unexpectedly into our haven while we were defending the walls. When they had taken our harbour, the wild soldiers wanted to plunder the village and our ships—one had already ravished a girl—but Cecrops would not permit it; and the Tyrian sailors, who still had Frisian blood in their veins, said, If you do that we will burn our ships, and you shall never see your mountains again. Cecrops, who had no inclination towards murder or devastation, sent messengers to Geert, requiring her to give up the citadel, offering her free exit with all her live and dead property, and her followers the same. The wisest of the citizens, seeing that they could not hold the citadel, advised Geert to accept at once, before Cecrops became furious and changed his mind. Three months afterwards Geert departed with the best of Frya's sons, and seven times twelve ships. Soon after they had left the harbour they fell in with at least thirty ships coming from Tyre with women and children. They were on their way to Athens, but when they heard how things stood there they went with Geert. The sea-king of the Tyrians brought them altogether through the strait which at that time ran into the Red Sea (now re-established as the Suez Canal). At last they landed at the Punjab, called in our language the Five Rivers, because five rivers flow together to the sea. Here they settled, and called it Geertmania. The King of Tyre afterwards, seeing that all his best sailors were gone, sent all his ships with his wild soldiers to catch them, dead or alive. When they arrived at the strait, both the sea and the earth trembled. The land was upheaved so that all the water ran out of the strait, and the muddy shores were raised up like a rampart. This happened on account of the virtues of the Geertmen, as every one can plainly understand.

In the Year One Thousand and Five after Atland was Submerged, This was Inscribed on the Eastern Wall of Fryasburgt

After twelve years had elapsed without our seeing any Italians in Almanland, there came three ships, finer than any that we possessed or had ever seen.

On the largest of them was a king of the Jonischen Islands whose name was Ulysses, the fame of whose wisdom was great. To him a priestess had prophesied that he should become the king of all Italy provided he could obtain a lamp that had been lighted at the lamp in Texland. For this purpose he had brought great treasures with him, above all, jewels for women more beautiful than had ever been seen before. They were from Troy, a town that the Greeks had taken. All these treasures he offered to the mother, but the mother would have nothing to do with them. At last, when he found that there was nothing to be got from her, he went to Walhallagara (Walcheren). There there was established a Burgtmaagd whose name was Kaat, but who was commonly called Kalip, because her lower lip stuck out like a mast-head. Here he tarried for years, to the scandal of all that knew it. According to the report of the maidens, he obtained a lamp from her; but it did him no good, because when he got to sea his ship was lost, and he was taken up naked and destitute by another ship. There was left behind by this king a writer of pure Frya's blood, born in the new harbour of Athens, who wrote for us what follows about Athens, from which may be seen how truly the mother Hel-licht spoke when she said that the customs of Frya could never take firm hold in Athens.

From the other Greeks you will have heard a great deal of bad about Cecrops, because he was not in good repute; but I dare affirm that he was an enlightened man; very renowned both among the inhabitants and among us, for he was against oppression, unlike the other priests, and was virtuous, and knew how to value the wisdom of distant nations. Knowing that, he permitted us to live according to our own Asegaboek. There was a story current that he was favourable to us because he was the son of a Frisian girl and an Egyptian priest: the reason of this was that he had blue eyes, and that many of our girls had been stolen and sold to Egypt, but he never confirmed this. However it may have been, certain it is that he showed us more friendship than all the other priests together. When he died, his successors soon began to tear up our charters, and gradually to enact so many unsuitable statutes that at long last nothing remained of liberty but the shadow and the name. Besides, they would not allow the laws to be written, so that the knowledge of them was hidden from us. Formerly all the cases in Athens were pleaded in our language, but afterwards in both languages, and at last in the native language only. At first the men of Athens only married women of our own race, but the young men as they grew up with the girls of the country took them to wife. The bastard children of this connection were the handsomest and cleverest in the world; but they were likewise the wickedest, wavering between the two parties, paying no regard to laws or customs except where they suited their own interests. As long as a ray of Frya's spirit existed, all the building materials were for common use, and no one might build a house larger or better than his neighbours; but when some degenerate townspeople got rich by sea-voyages and by the silver that their slaves got in the silver countries, they went to live out on the hills or in the valleys. There, behind high enclosures of trees or walls, they built palaces with costly furniture, and in order to remain in good odour with the nasty priests, they placed there likenesses of false gods and unchaste statues. Sometimes the dirty priests and princes wished for the boys rather than the girls, and often led them astray from the paths of virtue by rich presents or by force. Because riches were more valued by this lost and degenerate race than virtue or honour, one sometimes saw boys dressed in splendid flowing robes, to the disgrace of their parents and maidens, and to the shame of their own sex. If our simple parents came to a general assembly at Athens and made complaints, a cry was raised, Hear, hear! there is a sea-monster going to speak. Such is Athens become, like a morass in a tropical country full of leeches, toads, and poisonous snakes, in which no man of decent habits can set his foot.

This is Inscribed in All Our Citadels

How our Denmark was lost to us 1602 years after the submersion of Atland. Through the mad wantonness of Wodin, Magy had become master of the east part of Scandinavia. They dare not come over the hills and over the sea. The mother would not prevent it. She said, I see no danger in their weapons, but much in taking the Scandinavians back again, because they are so degenerate and spoilt. The general assembly were of the same opinion. Therefore it was left to him. A good hundred years ago Denmark began to trade; they gave their iron weapons in exchange for gold ornaments, as well as for copper and iron-ore. The mother sent messengers to advise them to have nothing to do with this trade. There was danger to their morals in it, and if they lost their morals they would soon lose their liberty. But the Denmarkers paid no attention to her. They did not believe that they could lose their morals, therefore they would not listen to her. At last they were at a loss themselves for weapons and necessaries, and this difficulty was their punishment. Their bodies were brilliantly adorned, but their cupboards and their sheds were empty. Just one hundred years after the first ship with provisions sailed from the coast, poverty and want made their appearance, hunger spread her wings all over the country, dissension marched proudly about the streets and into the houses, charity found no place, and unity departed. The child asked its mother for food; she had no food to give, only jewels. The women applied to their husbands, the husbands appealed to the counts; the counts had nothing to give, or if they had, they hid it away. Now the jewels must be sold, but while the sailors were away for that purpose, the frost came and laid a plank upon the sea and the strait (the Sound). When the frost had made the bridge, vigilance ceased in the land, and treachery took its place. Instead of watching on the shores, they put their horses in their sledges and drove off to Scandinavia. Then the Scandinavians, who hungered after the land of their forefathers, came to Denmark. One bright night they all came. Now, they said, we have a right to the land of our fathers; and while they were fighting about it, the Finns came to the defenceless villages and ran away with the children. As they had no good weapons, they lost the battle, and with it their freedom, and Magy became master. All this was the consequence of their not reading Frya's Tex, and neglecting her counsels. There are some who think that they were betrayed by the counts, and that the maidens had long suspected it; but if any one attempted to speak about it, his mouth was shut by golden chains.

We can express no opinion about it, we can only say to you, Do not trust too much to the wisdom of your princes or of your maidens; but if you wish to keep things straight, everybody must watch over his own passions, as well as the general welfare.

Two years afterwards Magy himself came with a fleet of light boats to steal the lamp from the mother of Texland. This wicked deed he accomplished one stormy winter night, while the wind roared and the hail rattled against the windows. The watchman on the tower hearing the noise, lighted his torch. As soon as the light from the tower fell upon the bastion, he saw that already armed men had got over the wall.

He immediately gave the alarm, but it was too late. Before the guard was ready, there were two thousand people battering the gate. The struggle did not last long. As the guard had not kept a good watch, they were overwhelmed. While the fight was going on, a rascally Finn stole into the chamber of the mother, and would have done her violence. She resisted him, and threw him down against the wall. When he got up, he ran his sword through her: If you will not have me, you shall have my sword. A Danish soldier came behind him and clave his head in two. There came from it a stream of black blood and a wreath of blue flame.

The Magy had the mother nursed on his own ship. As soon as she was well enough to speak clearly, the Magy told her that she must sail with him, but that she should keep her lamp and her maidens, and should hold a station higher than she had ever done before. Moreover, he said that he should ask her, in presence of all his chief men, if he would become the ruler of all the country and people of Frya; that she must declare and affirm this, or he would let her die a painful death. Then, when he had gathered all his chiefs around her bed, he asked, in a loud voice, Frana, since you are a prophetess, shall I become ruler over all the lands and people of Frya? Frana did as if she took no notice of him; but at last she opened her lips, and said: My eyes are dim, but the other light dawns upon my soul. Yes, I see it. Hear, Irtha, and rejoice with me. At the time of the submersion of Atland, the first spoke of the Juul stood at the top. After that it went down, and our freedom with it. When two spokes, or two thousand years, shall have rolled down, the sons shall arise who have been bred of the fornication of the princes and priests with the people, and shall witness against their fathers. They shall all fall by murder, but what they have proclaimed shall endure, and shall bear fruit in the bosoms of able men, like good seed which is laid in thy lap. Yet a thousand years shall the spoke descend, and sink deeper in darkness, and in the blood shed over you by the wickedness of the princes and priests. After that, the dawn shall begin to glow. When they perceive this, the false princes and priests will strive and wrestle against freedom; but freedom, love, and unity will take the people under their protection, and rise out of the vile pool. The light which at first only glimmered shall gradually become a flame. The blood of the bad shall flow over your surface, but you must not absorb it. At last the poisoned animals shall eat it, and die of it. All the stories that have been written in praise of the princes and priests shall be committed to the flames. Thenceforth your children shall live in peace. When she had finished speaking she sank down.

The Magy, who had not understood her, shrieked out, I have asked you if I should become master of all the lands and people of Frya, and now you have been speaking to another. Frana raised herself up, stared at him, and said, Before seven days have passed your soul shall haunt the tombs with the night-birds, and your body shall be at the bottom of the sea. Very good, said the Magy, swelling with rage; say that I am coming. Then he said to his executioners, Throw this woman overboard. This was the end of the last of the mothers. We do not ask for revenge. Time will provide that; but a thousand thousand times we will call with Frya, Watch! watch! watch!

How it Fared Afterwards with the Magy

After the murder of the mother, he brought the lamp and the maidens into his own ship, together with all the booty that he chose. Afterwards he went up the Flymeer because he wished to take the maiden of Medeasblik or Stavoren and install her as mother; but there they were on their guard. The seafaring men of Stavoren and Alderga would gladly have gone to Jon, but the great fleet was out on a distant voyage; so they proceeded in their small fleet to Medeasblik, and kept themselves concealed in a sheltered place behind trees. The Magy approached Medeasblik in broad daylight; nevertheless, his men boldly stormed the citadel. But as they landed from the boats, our people sallied forth from the creek, and shot their arrows with balls of burning turpentine upon the fleet. They were so well aimed that many of the ships were instantly on fire. Those left to guard the ships shot at us, but they could not reach us. When at last a burning ship drifted towards the ship of the Magy, he ordered the man at the helm to sheer off, but this man was the Dane who had cleft the head of the Finn. He said, You sent our Eeremoeder to the bottom of the sea to say that you were coming. In the bustle of the fight you might forget it; now I will take care that you keep your word. The Magy tried to push him off, but the sailor, a real Frisian and strong as an ox, clutched his head with both hands, and pitched him into the surging billows. Then he hoisted up his brown shield, and sailed straight to our fleet. Thus the maidens came unhurt to us; but the lamp was extinguished, and no one knew how that had happened. When those on the uninjured ships heard that the Magy was drowned, they sailed away, because their crews were Danes. When the fleet was far enough off, our sailors turned and shot their burning arrows at the Finns. When the Finns saw that, and found that they were betrayed, they fell into confusion, and lost all discipline and order. At this moment the garrison sallied forth from the citadel. Those who resisted were killed, and those who fled found their death in the marshes of the Krylinger wood.

Postscript

When the sailors were in the creek, there was a wag from Stavoren among them, who said, Medea may well laugh if we rescue her from her citadel. Upon this, the maidens gave to the creek the name Medea mêilakkia (Lake of Medea). The occurrences that happened after this everybody can remember. The maidens ought to relate it in their own way, and have it well inscribed. We consider that our task is fulfilled. Hail!

The End of the Book.

The Writings of Adelbrost and Apollonia

My name is Adelbrost, the son of Apol and Adela. I was elected by my people as Grevetman over the Lindaoorden. Therefore I will continue this book in the same way as my mother has spoken it.

After the Magy was killed and Fryasburgt was restored, a mother had to be chosen. The mother had not named her successor, and her will was nowhere to be found. Seven months later a general assembly was called at Grênegâ (Groningen), because it was on the boundary of Saxamarken. My mother was chosen, but she would not be the mother. She had saved my father's life, in consequence of which they had fallen in love with each other, and she wished to marry. Many people wished my mother to alter her decision, but she said an Eeremoeder ought to be as pure in her conscience as she appears outwardly, and to have the same love for all her children. Now, as I love Apol better than anything else in the world, I cannot be such a mother. Thus spoke and reasoned Adela, but all the other maidens wished to be the mother. Each state was in favour of its own maiden, and would not yield. Therefore none was chosen, and the kingdom was without any restraint. From what follows you will understand Liudgert, the king who had lately died, had been chosen in the lifetime of the mother, and seemingly with the love and confidence of all the states. It was his turn to live at the great court of Dokhem, and in the lifetime of the mother great honour was done to him there, as there were more messengers and knights there than had ever been seen there before. But now he was lonely and forsaken, because every one was afraid that he would set himself above the law, and rule them like the slave kings. Every headman imagined that he did enough if he looked after his own state, and did not care for the others. With the Burgtmaagden it was still worse. Each of them depended upon her own judgment, and whenever a Grevetman did anything without her, she raised distrust between him and his people. If any case happened which concerned several states, and one maid had been consulted, the rest all exclaimed that she had spoken only in the interest of her own state. By such proceedings they brought disputes among the states, and so severed the bond of union that the people of one state were jealous of those of the rest, or at least considered them as strangers; the consequence of which was that the Gauls or Truwenden (Druids) took possession of our lands as far as the Scheldt, and the Magy as far as the Wesara. How this happened my mother has explained, otherwise this book would not have been written, although I have lost all hope that it would be of any use. I do not write in the hope that I shall win back the land or preserve it: in my opinion that is impossible. I write only for the future generations, that they may all know in what way we were lost, and that each may learn that every crime brings its punishment.

My name is Apollonia. Two-and-thirty days after my mother's death my brother Adelbrost was found murdered on the wharf, his skull fractured and his limbs torn asunder. My father, who lay ill, died of fright. Then my younger brother, Apol, sailed from here to the west side of Schoonland. There he built a citadel named Lindasburgt, in order there to avenge our wrong. Wr-alda accorded him many years for that. He had five sons, who all caused fear to Magy, and brought fame to my brother. After the death of my mother and my brother, all the bravest of the land joined together and made a covenant, called the Adelbond. In order to preserve us from injury, they brought me and my youngest brother, Adelhirt, to the burgt—me to the maidens, and him to the warriors. When I was thirty years old I was chosen as Burgtmaagd, and my brother at fifty was chosen Grevetman. From mother's side my brother was the sixth, but from father's side the third. By right, therefore, his descendants could not put "overa Linda" after their names, but they all wished to do it in honour of their mother. In addition to this, there was given to us also a copy of "The Book of Adela's Followers." That gave me the most pleasure, because it came into the world by my mother's wisdom. In the burgt I have found other writings also in praise of my mother. All this I will write afterwards.

These are the writings left by Bruno, who was the writer of this burgt. After the followers of Adela had made copies, each in his kingdom, of what was inscribed upon the walls of the burgt, they resolved to choose a mother. For this purpose a general assembly was called at this farm. By the first advice of Adela, Teuntje was recommended. That would have been arranged, only that my Burgtmaagd asked to speak: she had always supposed that she would be chosen mother, because she was at the burgt from which mothers had generally been chosen. When she was allowed to speak, she opened her false lips and said: You all seem to place great value on Adela's advice, but that shall not shut my mouth. Who is Adela, and whence comes it that you respect her so highly? She was what I am now, a Burgtmaagd of this place; is she, then, wiser and better than I and all the others? or is she more conversant with our laws and customs? If that had been the case, she would have become mother when she was chosen; but instead of that, she preferred matrimony to a single life, watching over herself and her people. She is certainly very clear-sighted, but my eyes are far from being dim. I have observed that she is very much attached to her husband, which is very praiseworthy; but I see, likewise, that Teuntje is Apol's niece. Further I say nothing.

The principal people understood very well which way the wind blew with her; but among the people there arose disputes, and as most of the people came from here, they would not give the honour to Teuntje. The conferences were ended, knives were drawn, and no mother was chosen. Shortly afterwards one of our messengers killed his comrade. As he had been a man of good character hitherto, my Burgtmaagd had permission to help him over the frontier; but instead of helping him over to Twiskland (Germany), she fled with him herself to Wesara, and then to the Magy. The Magy, who wished to please his sons of Frya, appointed her mother of Godaburgt, in Schoonland; but she wished for more, and she told him that if he could get Adela out of the way he might become master of the whole of Frya's land. She said she hated Adela for having prevented her from being chosen mother. If he would promise her Texland, her messenger should serve as guide to his warriors. All this was confessed by her messenger.

The Second Writing

Fifteen months after the last general assembly, at the festival of the harvest month, everybody gave himself up to pleasure and merry-making, and no one thought of anything but diversion; but Wr-alda wished to teach us that watchfulness should never be relaxed. In the midst of the festivities the fog came and enveloped every place in darkness. Cheerfulness melted away, but watchfulness did not take its place. The coastguard deserted their beacons, and no one was to be seen on any of the paths. When the fog rose, the sun scarcely appeared among the clouds; but the people all came out shouting with joy, and the young folks went about singing to their bagpipes, filling the air with their melody. But while every one was intoxicated with pleasure, treachery had landed with its horses and riders. As usual, darkness had favoured the wicked, and they had slipped in through the paths of Linda's wood. Before Adela's door twelve girls led twelve lambs, and twelve boys led twelve calves. A young Saxon bestrode a wild bull which he had caught and tamed. They were decked with all kinds of flowers, and the girls' dresses were fringed with gold from the Rhine.

When Adela came out of her house, a shower of flowers fell on her head; they all cheered loudly, and the fifes of the boys were heard over everything. Poor Adela! poor people! how short will be your joy! When the procession was out of sight, a troop of Magyar soldiers rushed up to Adela's house. Her father and her husband were sitting on the steps. The door was open, and within stood Adelbrost her son. When he saw the danger of his parents, he took his bow from the wall and shot the leader of the pirates, who staggered and fell on the grass. The second and third met a similar fate. In the meantime his parents had seized their weapons, and went slowly to Jon's house. They would soon have been taken, but Adela came. She had learned in the burgt to use all kinds of weapons. She was seven feet high, and her sword was the same length. She waved it three times over her head, and each time a knight bit the earth. Reinforcements came, and the pirates were made prisoners; but too late—an arrow had penetrated her bosom! The treacherous Magy had poisoned it, and she died of it.

The Elegy of the Burgtmaagd

Yes, departed friend, thousands are arrived, and more are coming. They wish to hear the wisdom of Adela. Truly, she was a princess, for she had always been the leader. O Sorrow, what good can you do!

Her garments of linen and wool she spun and wove herself. How could she add to her beauty? Not with pearls, for her teeth were more white; not with gold, for her tresses were more brilliant; not with precious stones, for her eyes, though soft as those of a lamb, were so lustrous that you could scarcely look into them. But why do I talk of beauty? Frya was certainly not more beautiful; yes, my friends, Frya, who possessed seven perfections, of which each of her daughters inherited one, or at most three. But even if she had been ugly, she would still have been dear to us. Is she warlike? Listen, my friend. Adela was the only daughter of our Grevetman. She stood seven feet high. Her wisdom exceeded her stature, and her courage was equal to both together. Here is an instance. There was once a turf-ground on fire. Three children got upon yonder gravestone. There was a furious wind. The people were all shouting, and the mother was helpless. Then came Adela. What are you all standing still here for? she cried. Try to help them, and

Wr-alda will give you strength. Then she ran to the Krylwood and got some elder branches, of which she made a bridge. The others then came to assist her, and the children were saved. The children bring flowers to the place every year. There came once three Phœnician sailors, who began to ill-treat the children, when Adela, having heard their screams, beat the scoundrels till they were insensible, and then, to prove to them what miserable wretches they were, she tied them all three to a spindle.

The foreign lords came to look after their people, and when they saw how ridiculously they had been treated they were very angry, till they were told what had happened. Upon that they bowed themselves before Adela, and kissed the hem of her garment. But come, distant living friend. The birds of the forest fled before the numerous visitors. Come, friend, and you shall hear her wisdom. By the gravestone of which mention has already been made her body is buried. Upon the stone the following words are inscribed:—

Tread softly, for here lies Adela.

The old legend which is written on the outside wall of the city tower is not written in "The Book of Adela's Followers." Why this has been neglected I do not know; but this book is my own, so I will put it in out of regard to my relations.

The Oldest Doctrine

Hail to all the well-intentioned children of Frya! Through them the earth shall become holy. Learn and announce to the people Wr-alda is the ancient of ancients, for he created all things. Wr-alda is all in all, for he is eternal and everlasting. Wr-alda is omnipresent but invisible, and therefore is called a spirit. All that we can see of him are the created beings who come to life through him and go again, because from Wr-alda all things proceed and return to him. Wr-alda is the beginning and the end. Wr-alda is the only almighty being, because from him all other strength comes, and returns to him. Therefore he alone is the creator, and nothing exists without him. Wr-alda established eternal principles, upon which the laws of creation were founded, and no good laws could stand on any other foundation. But although everything is derived from Wr-alda, the wickedness of men does not come from him. Wickedness comes from heaviness, carelessness, and stupidity; therefore they may well be injurious to men, but never to Wr-alda. Wr-alda is wisdom, and the laws that he has made are the books from which we learn, nor is any wisdom to be found or gathered but in them. Men may see a great deal, but Wr-alda sees everything. Men can learn a great deal, but Wr-alda knows everything. Men can discover much, but to Wr-alda everything is open. Mankind are male and female, but Wr-alda created both. Mankind love and hate, but Wr-alda alone is just. Therefore

Wr-alda is good, and there is no good without him. In the progress of time all creation alters and changes, but goodness alone is unalterable; and since Wr-alda is good, he cannot change. As he endures, he alone exists; everything else is show.

The Second Part of the Oldest Doctrine

Among Finda's people there are false teachers, who, by their over-inventiveness, have become so wicked that they make themselves and their adherents believe that they are the best part of Wr-alda, that their spirit is the best part of Wr-alda's spirit, and that Wr-alda can only think by the help of their brains.

That every creature is a part of Wr-alda's eternal being, that they have stolen from us; but their false reasoning and ungovernable pride have brought them on the road to ruin. If their spirit was Wr-alda's spirit, then Wr-alda would be very stupid, instead of being sensible and wise; for their spirit labours to create beautiful statues, which they afterwards worship. Finda's people are a wicked people, for although they presumptuously pretend among themselves that they are gods, they proclaim the unconsecrated false gods, and declare everywhere that these idols created the world and all that therein is—greedy idols, full of envy and anger, who desire to be served and honoured by the people, and who exact bloody sacrifices and rich offerings; but these presumptuous and false men, who call themselves God's servants and priests, receive and collect everything in the name of the idols that have no real existence, for their own benefit.

They do all this with an easy conscience, as they think themselves gods not answerable to any one. If there are some who discover their tricks and expose them, they hand them over to the executioners to be burnt for their calumnies, with solemn ceremonies in honour of the false gods; but really in order to save themselves. In order that our children may be protected against their idolatrous doctrine, the duty of the maidens is to make them learn by heart the following: Wr-alda existed before all things, and will endure after all things. Wr-alda is also eternal and everlasting, therefore nothing exists without him. From Wr-alda's life sprang time and all living things, and his life takes away time and every other thing. These things must be made clear and manifest in every way, so that they can be made clear and comprehensible to all. When we have learned thus much, then we say further: In what regards our existence, we are a part of Wr-alda's everlasting being, like the existence of all created beings; but as regards our form, our qualities, our spirit, and all our thoughts, these do not belong to the being. All these are passing things which appear through Wr-alda's life, and which appear through his wisdom, and not otherwise; but whereas his life is continually progressing, nothing can remain stationary, therefore all created things change their locality, their form, and their thoughts. So neither the earth nor any other created object can say, I am; but rather, I was. So no man can say, I think; but rather, I thought. The boy is greater and different from the child; he has different desires, inclinations, and thoughts. The man and father feels and thinks differently from the boy, the old man just the same. Everybody knows that. Besides, everybody knows and must acknowledge that he is now changing, that he changes every minute even while he says, I am, and that his thoughts change even while he says, I think. Instead, then, of imitating Finda's wicked people, and saying, I am the best part of Wr-alda, and through us alone he can think, we proclaim everywhere where it is necessary, We, Frya's children, exist through Wr-alda's life—in the beginning mean and base, but always advancing towards perfection without ever attaining the excellence of Wr-alda himself. Our spirit is not Wr-alda's spirit, it is merely a shadow of it. When Wr-alda created us, he lent us his wisdom, brains, organs, memory, and many other good qualities. By this means we are able to contemplate his creatures and his laws; by this means we can learn and can speak of them always, and only for our own benefit. If Wr-alda had given us no organs, we should have known nothing, and been more irrational than a piece of sea-weed driven up and down by the ebb and flood.

This is Written on Parchment—"Skrivfilt." Speech and Answer to other Maidens as an Example

An unsociable, avaricious man came to complain to Troost, who was the maid of Stavia. He said a thunderstorm had destroyed his house. He had prayed to Wr-alda, but Wr-alda had given him no help. Are you a true Frisian? Troost asked. From father and forefathers, replied the man. Then she said, I will sow something in your conscience, in confidence that it will take root, grow, and bear fruit. She continued, When Frya was born, our mother stood naked and bare, unprotected from the rays of the sun. She could ask no one, and there was no one who could give her any help. Then Wr-alda wrought in her conscience inclination and love, anxiety and fright. She looked round her, and her inclination chose the best. She sought a hiding-place under the sheltering lime-trees, but the rain came, and the difficulty was that she got wet. She had seen how the water ran down the pendent leaves; so she made a roof of leaves fastened with sticks, but the wind blew the rain under it. She observed that the stem would afford protection. She then built a wall of sods, first on one side, and then all round. The wind grew stronger and blew away the roof, but she made no complaint of Wr-alda. She made a roof of rushes, and put stones upon it. Having found how hard it is to toil alone, she showed her children how and why she had done it. They acted and thought as she did. This is the way in which we became possessed of houses and porches, a street, and lime-trees to protect us from the rays of the sun. At last we have built a citadel, and all the rest. If your house is not strong enough, then you must try and make another. My house was strong enough, he said, but the flood and the wind destroyed it. Where did your house stand? Troost asked. On the bank of the Rhine, he answered. Did it not stand on a knoll? Troost asked. No, said the man; my house stood alone on the bank. I built it alone, but I could not alone make a hillock. I knew it, Troost answered; the maidens told me. All your life you have avoided your neighbours, fearing that you might have to give or do something for them; but one cannot get on in the world in that way, for Wr-alda, who is kind, turns away from the niggardly. Fâsta has advised us, and it is engraved in stone over all our doors. If you are selfish, distrustful towards your neighbours, teach your neighbours, help your neighbours, and they will return the same to you. If this advice is not good enough for you, I can give you no better. The man blushed for shame, and slunk away.

Now I will Write Myself, First about My Citadel, and then about what I have been Able to See

My city lies near the north end of the Liudgaarde. The tower has six sides, and is ninety feet high, flat-roofed, with a small house upon it out of which they look at the stars. On either side of the tower is a house three hundred feet long, and twenty-one feet broad, and twenty-one feet high, besides the roof, which is round. All this is built of hard-baked bricks, and outside there is nothing else. The citadel is surrounded by a dyke, with a moat thirty-six feet broad and twenty-one feet deep. If one looks down from the tower, he sees the form of the Juul. In the ground among the houses on the south side all kinds of native and foreign herbs grow, of which the maidens must study the qualities. Among the houses on the north side there are only fields. The three houses on the north are full of corn and other necessaries; the two houses on the south are for the maidens to live in and keep school. The most southern house is the dwelling of the Burgtmaagd. In the tower hangs the lamp. The walls of the tower are decorated with precious stones. On the south wall the Tex is inscribed. On the right side of this are the formulae, and on the other side the laws; the other things are found upon the three other sides. Against the dyke, near the house of the Burgtmaagd, stand the oven and the mill, worked by four oxen. Outside the citadel wall is the place where the Burgtheeren and the soldiers live. The fortification outside is an hour long—not a seaman's hour, but an hour of the sun, of which twenty-four go to a day. Inside it is a plain five feet below the top. On it are three hundred crossbows covered with wood and leather.

Besides the houses of the inhabitants, there are along the inside of the dyke thirty-six refuge-houses for the people who live in the neighbourhood. The field serves for a camp and for a meadow. On the south side of the outer fortification is the Liudgaarde, enclosed by the great wood of lime-trees. Its shape is three-cornered, with the widest part outside, so that the sun may shine in it, for there are a great number of foreign trees and flowers brought by the seafarers. All the other citadels are the same shape as ours, only not so large; but the largest of all is that of Texland. The tower of the Fryaburgt is so high that it rends the sky, and all the rest is in proportion to the tower. In our citadel this is the arrangement: Seven young maidens attend to the lamp; each watch is three hours. In the rest of their time they do housework, learn, and sleep. When they have watched for seven years, they are free; then they may go among the people, to look after their morals and to give advice. When they have been three years maidens, they may sometimes accompany the older ones.

The writer must teach the girls to read, to write, and to reckon. The elders, or "Greva," must teach them justice and duty, morals, botany, and medicine, history, traditions, and singing, besides all that may be necessary for them to give advice. The Burgtmaagd must teach them how to set to work when they go among the people. Before a Burgtmaagd can take office, she must travel through the country a whole year. Three grey-headed Burgtheeren and three old maidens must go with her. This was the way that I did. My journey was along the Rhine—on this side up, and on the other side down. The higher I went, the poorer the people seemed to be. Everywhere about the Rhine the people dug holes, and the sand that was got out was poured with water over fleeces to get the gold, but the girls did not wear golden crowns of it. Formerly they were more numerous, but since we lost Schoonland they have gone up to the mountains. There they dig ore and make iron. Above the Rhine among the mountains I have seen Marsaten. The Marsaten are people who live on the lakes. Their houses are built upon piles, for protection from the wild beasts and wicked people. There are wolves, bears, and horrible lions. Then come the Swiss, the nearest to the frontiers of the distant Italians, the followers of Kalta and the savage Twiskar, all greedy for robbery and booty. The Marsaten gain their livelihood by fishing and hunting. The skins are sewn together by the women, and prepared with birch bark. The small skins are as soft as a woman's skin. The Burgtmaagd at Fryasburgt (Freiburg) told us that they were good, simple people; but if I had not heard her speak of them first, I should have thought that they were not Frya's people, they looked so impudent. Their wool and herbs are bought by the Rhine people, and taken to foreign countries by the ship captains. Along the other side of the Rhine it was just the same as at Lydasburcht (Leiden). There was a great river or lake, and upon this lake also there were people living upon piles. But they were not Frya's people; they were black and brown men who had been employed as rowers to bring home the men who had been making foreign voyages, and they had to stay there till the fleet went back.

At last we came to Alderga. At the head of the south harbour lies the Waraburgt, built of stone, in which all kinds of clothes, weapons, shells, and horns are kept, which were brought by the sea-people from distant lands. A quarter of an hour's distance from there is Alderga, a great river surrounded by houses, sheds, and gardens, all richly decorated. In the river lay a great fleet ready, with banners of all sorts of colours. On Frya's day the shields were hung on board likewise. Some shone like the sun. The shields of the sea-king and the admiral were bordered with gold. From the river a canal was dug going past the citadel Forana (Vroonen), with a narrow outlet to the sea. This was the egress of the fleet; the Fly was the ingress. On both sides of the river are fine houses built, painted in bright colours. The gardens are all surrounded by green hedges. I saw there women wearing felt tunics, as if it were writing felt.1 Just as at Staveren, the girls wore golden crowns on their heads, and rings on their arms and ankles. To the south of Forana lies Alkmarum. Alkmarum is a lake or river in which there is an island. On this island the black and brown people must remain, the same as at Lydasburgt. The Burgtmaagd of Forana told me that the burgtheeren go every day to teach them what real freedom is, and how it behoves men to live in order to obtain the blessing of Wr-alda's spirit. If there was any one who was willing to listen and could comprehend, he was kept there till he was fully taught. That was done in order to instruct the distant people, and to make friends everywhere. I had been before in the Saxenmarken, at the Mannagardaforde castle (Munster). There I saw more poverty than I could discover wealth here. She answered: So whenever at the Saxenmarken a young man courts a young girl, the girls ask: Can you keep your house free from the banished Twisklanders? Have you ever killed any of them? How many cattle have you already caught, and how many bear and wolfskins have you brought to market? And from this it comes that the Saxons have left the cultivation of the soil to the women, that not one in a hundred can read or write; from this it comes, too, that no one has a motto on his shield, but only a misshapen form of some animal that he has killed; and lastly, from this comes also that they are very warlike, but sometimes as stupid as the beasts that they catch, and as poor as the Twisklanders with whom they go to war. The earth and the sea were made for Frya's people. All our rivers run into the sea. The Lydas people and the Findas people will exterminate each other, and we must people the empty countries. In movement and sailing is our prosperity. If you wish the highlanders to share our riches and wisdom, I will give you a piece of advice. Let the girls, when they are asked to marry, before they say yes, ask their lovers: What parts of the world have you travelled in? What can you tell your children about distant lands and distant people? If they do this, then the young warriors will come to us; they will become wiser and richer, and we shall have no occasion to deal with those nasty people. The youngest of the maids who were with me came from the Saxenmarken. When we came back she asked leave to go home. Afterwards she became Burgtmaagd there, and that is the reason why in these days so many of our sailors are Saxons.

End of Apollonia's Book.

The Writings of Frêthorik and Wiljow

My name is Frêthorik, surnamed oera Linda, which means over the Linden. In Ljudwardia I was chosen as Asga. Ljudwardia is a new village within the fortification of the Ljudgaarda, of which the name has fallen into disrepute. In my time much has happened. I had written a good deal about it, but afterwards much more was related to me. I will write an account of both one and the other after this book, to the honour of the good people and to the disgrace of the bad.

In my youth I heard complaints on all sides. The bad time was coming; the bad time did come—Frya had forsaken us. She withheld from us all her watch-maidens, because monstrous idolatrous images had been found within our landmarks. I burnt with curiosity to see those images. In our neighbourhood a little old woman tottered in and out of the houses, always calling out about the bad times. I came to her; she stroked my chin; then I became bold, and asked her if she would show me the bad times and the images. She laughed good-naturedly, and took me to the citadel. An old man asked me if I could read and write. No, I said. Then you must first go and learn, he replied, otherwise it may not be shown to you. I went daily to the writer and learnt. Eight years afterwards I heard that our Burgtmaagd had been unchaste, and that some of the burgtheeren had committed treason with the Magy, and many people took their part. Everywhere disputes arose. There were children rebelling against their parents; good people were secretly murdered. The little old woman who had brought everything to light was found dead in a ditch. My father, who was a judge, would have her avenged. He was murdered in the night in his own house. Three years after that the Magy was master without any resistance. The Saxmen had remained religious and upright. All the good people fled to them. My mother died of it. Now I did like the others. The Magy prided himself upon his cunning, but Irtha made him know that she would not tolerate any Magy or idol on the holy bosom that had borne Frya. As a wild horse tosses his mane after he has thrown his rider, so Irtha shook her forests and her mountains. Rivers flowed over the land; the sea raged; mountains spouted fire to the clouds, and what they vomited forth the clouds flung upon the earth. At the beginning of the Arnemaand (harvest month) the earth bowed towards the north, and sank down lower and lower. In the Welvenmaand (winter month) the low lands of Fryasland were buried under the sea. The woods in which the images were, were torn up and scattered by the wind. The following year the frost came in the Hardemaand (Louwmaand, January), and laid Fryasland concealed under a sheet of ice. In Sellemaand (Sprokkelmaand, February) there were storms of wind from the north, driving mountains of ice and stones. When the spring-tides came the earth raised herself up, the ice melted; with the ebb the forests with the images drifted out to sea. In the Winne, or Minnemaand (Bloeimaand, May), every one who dared went home. I came with a maiden to the citadel Liudgaarde. How sad it looked there. The forests of the Lindaoorden were almost all gone. Where Liudgaarde used to be was sea. The waves swept over the fortifications. Ice had destroyed the tower, and the houses lay heaped over each other. On the slope of the dyke I found a stone on which the writer had inscribed his name. That was a sign to me. The same thing had happened to other citadels as to ours. In the upper lands they had been destroyed by the earth, in the lower lands by the water. Fryasburgt, at Texland, was the only one found uninjured, but all the land to the north was sunk under the sea, and has never been recovered. At the mouth of the Flymeer, as we were told, thirty salt swamps were found, consisting of the forest and the ground that had been swept away. At Westflyland there were fifty. The canal which had run across the land from Alderga was filled up with sand and destroyed. The seafaring people and other travellers who were at home had saved themselves, their goods, and their relations upon their ships. But the black people at Lydasburgt and Alkmarum had done the same; and as they went south they saved many girls, and as no one came to claim them, they took them for their wives. The people who came back all lived within the lines of the citadel, as outside there was nothing but mud and marsh. The old houses were all smashed together. People bought cattle and sheep from the upper lands, and in the great houses where formerly the maidens were established cloth and felt were made for a livelihood. This happened 1888 years after the submersion of Atland.

For 282 years we had not had an Eeremoeder, and now, when everything seemed lost, they set about choosing one. The lot fell upon Gosa, surnamed Makonta. She was Burgtmaagd at Fryasburgt, in Texland. She had a clear head and strong sense, and was very good; and as her citadel was the only one that had been spared, every one saw in that her call. Ten years after that the seafarers came from Forana and Lydasburgt. They wished to drive the black men, with their wives and children, out of the country. They wished to obtain the opinion of the mother upon the subject. She asked them: Can you send them all back to their country? If so, then lose no time, or they will find no relatives alive. No, they said. Gosa replied: They have eaten your bread and salt; they have placed themselves entirely under your protection. You must consult your own hearts. But I will give you one piece of advice. Keep them till you are able to send them back, but keep them outside your citadels. Watch over their morals, and educate them as if they were Frya's sons. Their women are the strongest here. Their blood will disappear like smoke, till at last nothing but Frya's blood will remain in their descendants. So they remained here. Now, I should wish that my descendants should observe in how far Gosa spoke the truth. When our country began to recover, there came troops of poor Saxon men and women to the neighbourhoods of Staveren and Alderga, to search for gold and other treasures in the swampy lands. But the sea-people would not permit it, so they went and settled in the empty village of the West Flyland in order to preserve their lives.

Now I Will Relate how the Geertman and Many Followers of Hellenia Came Back

Two years after Gosa had become the mother (303 B.C.) there arrived a fleet at Flymeer. The people shouted "Ho-n-sêen" (What a blessing). They sailed to Staveren, where they shouted again. Their flags were hoisted, and at night they shot lighted arrows into the air. At daylight some of them rowed into the harbour in a boat, shouting again, "Ho-n-sêen." When they landed a young fellow jumped upon the rampart. In his hand he held a shield on which bread and salt were laid. After him came a grey-headed man, who said we come from the distant Greek land to preserve our customs. Now we wish you to be kind enough to give us as much land as will enable us to live. He told a long story, which I will hereafter relate more fully. The old man did not know what to do. They sent messengers all round, also to me. I went, and said now that we have a mother it behoves us to ask her advice. I went with them myself. The mother, who already knew it all, said: Let them come, they will help us to keep our lands, but do not let them remain in one place, that they may not become too powerful over us. We did as she said, which was quite to their liking. Fryso remained with his people at Staveren, which they made again into a port as well as they could. Wichhirte went with his people eastwards to the Emude. Some of the descendants of Jon who imagined that they sprang from the Alderga people went there. A small number, who fancied that their forefathers had come from the seven islands, went there and set themselves down within the enclosure of the citadel of Walhallagara. Liudgert, the admiral of

Wichhirt, was my comrade, and afterwards my friend. Out of his diary I have taken the following history.

After we had been settled 12 times 100 and twice 12 years in the Five Waters (Punjab), whilst our naval warriors were navigating all the seas they could find, came Alexander the King, with a powerful army descending the river towards our villages. No one could withstand him; but we sea-people, who lived by the sea, put all our possessions on board ships and took our departure. When Alexander heard that such a large fleet had escaped him, he became furious, and swore that he would burn all the villages if we did not come back. Wichhirte was ill in bed. When Alexander heard that, he waited till he was better. After that he came to him, speaking very kindly—but he deceived, as he had done before. Wichhirte answered: Oh greatest of kings, we sailors go everywhere; we have heard of your great deeds, therefore we are full of respect for your arms, and still more for your wisdom; but we who are free-born Fryas children, we may not become your slaves; and even if I would, the others would sooner die, for so it is commanded in our laws. Alexander said: I do not desire to take your land or make slaves of your people, I only wish to hire your services. That I will swear by both our Gods, so that no one may be dissatisfied. When Alexander shared bread and salt with him, Wichhirte had chosen the wisest part. He let his son fetch the ships. When they were all come back Alexander hired them all. By means of them he wished to transport his people to the holy Ganges, which he had not been able to reach. Then he chose among all his people and soldiers those who were accustomed to the sea. Wichhirte had fallen sick again, therefore I went alone with Nearchus, sent by the king. The voyage came to an end without any advantage, because the Joniers and the Phœnicians were always quarrelling, so that Nearchus himself could not keep them in order. In the meantime, the king had not sat still. He had let his soldiers cut down trees and make planks, with which, with the help of our carpenters, he had built ships. Now he would himself become a sea-king, and sail with his whole army up the Ganges; but the soldiers who came from the mountainous countries were afraid of the sea. When they heard that they must sail, they set fire to the timber yards, and so our whole village was laid in ashes. At first we thought that this had been done by Alexander's orders, and we were all ready to cast ourselves into the sea: but Alexander was furious, and wished his own people to kill the soldiers. However, Nearchus, who was not only his chief officer, but also his friend, advised him not to do so. So he pretended to believe that it had happened by accident, and said no more about it. He wished now to return, but before going he made an inquiry who really were the guilty ones. As soon as he ascertained it, he had them all disarmed, and made them build a new village. His own people he kept under arms to overawe the others, and to build a citadel. We were to take the women and children with us. When we arrived at the mouth of the Euphrates, we might either choose a place to settle there or come back. Our pay would be guaranteed to us the same in either case. Upon the new ships which had been saved from the fire he embarked the Joniers and the Greeks. He himself went with the rest of his people along the coast, through the barren wilderness; that is, through the land that Irtha had heaved up out of the sea when she had raised up the strait as soon as our forefathers had passed into the Red Sea.

When we arrived at New Gertmania (New Gertmania is the port that we had made in order to take in water), we met Alexander with his army. Nearchus went ashore, and stayed three days. Then we proceeded further on. When we came to the Euphrates, Nearchus went ashore with the soldiers and a large body of people; but he soon returned, and said, The King requests you, for his sake, to go a voyage up the Red Sea; after that each shall receive as much gold as he can carry. When we arrived there, he showed us where the strait had formerly been. There he spent thirty-one days, always looking steadily towards the desert.

At last there arrived a great troop of people, bringing with them 200 elephants, 1000 camels, a quantity of timber, ropes, and all kinds of implements necessary to drag our fleet to the Mediterranean Sea. This astounded us, and seemed most extraordinary; but Nearchus told us that his king wished to show to the other kings that he was more powerful than any kings of Tyre had ever been. We were only to assist, and that surely could do us no harm. We were obliged to yield, and Nearchus knew so well how to regulate everything, that before three months had elapsed our ships lay in the Mediterranean Sea. When Alexander ascertained how his project had succeeded, he became so audacious that he wished to dig out the dried-up strait in defiance of Irtha; but Wr-alda deserted his soul, so that he destroyed himself by wine and rashness before he could begin it. After his death his kingdom was divided among his princes. They were each to have preserved a share for his sons, but that was not their intention. Each wished to keep his own share, and to get more. Then war arose, and we could not return. Nearchus wished us to settle on the coast of Phœnicia, but that no one would do. We said we would rather risk the attempt to return to Fryasland. Then he brought us to the new port of Athens, where all the true children of Frya had formerly gone. We went, soldiers with our goods and weapons. Among the many princes Nearchus had a friend named Antigonus. These two had only one object in view, as they told us—to help the royal race, and to restore freedom to all the Greek lands. Antigonus had, among many others, one son named Demetrius, afterwards called the "City Winner." He went once to the town of Salamis, and after he had been some time fighting there, he had an engagement with the fleet of Ptolemy. Ptolemy was the name of the prince who reigned over Egypt. Demetrius won the battle, not by his own soldiers, but because we helped him. We had done this out of friendship for Nearchus, because we knew that he was of bastard birth by his white skin, blue eyes, and fair hair. Afterwards, Demetrius attacked Rhodes, and we transported thither his soldiers and provisions. When we made our last voyage to Rhodes, the war was finished. Demetrius had sailed to Athens. When we came into the harbour, the whole village was in deep mourning. Friso, who was king over the fleet, had a son and a daughter so remarkably fair, as if they had just come out of Fryasland, and more beautiful than any one could picture to himself. The fame of this went all over Greece, and came to the ears of Demetrius. Demetrius was vile and immoral, and thought he could do as he pleased. He carried off the daughter. The mother did not dare await the return of her joi (the sailors wives call their husbands joi or zoethart (sweetheart). The men call their wives troost (comfort) and fro or frow, that is, vreuyde (delight) and frolic; that is the same as vreugde.)

As she dared not wait for her husband's return, she went with her son to Demetrius, and implored him to send back her daughter; but when Demetrius saw the son he had him taken to his palace, and did to him as he had done to his sister. He sent a bag of gold to the mother, which she flung into the sea. When she came home she was out of her mind, and ran about the streets calling out: Have you seen my children. Woe is me! let me find a place to hide in, for my husband will kill me because I have lost his children.

When Demetrius heard that Friso had come home, he sent messengers to him to say that he had taken his children to raise them to high rank, and to reward him for his services. But Friso was proud and passionate, and sent a messenger with a letter to his children, in which he recommended them to accept the will of Demetrius, as he wished to promote their happiness; but the messenger had another letter with poison, which he ordered them to take: But, said he, your bodies have been defiled against your will. That you are not to blame for; but if your souls are not pure, you will never come into Walhalla. Your spirits will haunt the earth in darkness. Like the bats and owls, you will hide yourselves in the daytime in holes, and in the night will come and shriek and cry about our graves, while Frya must turn her head away from you. The children did as their father had commanded. The messenger had their bodies thrown into the sea, and it was reported that they had fled. Now Friso wished to go with all his people to Frya's land, where he had been formerly, but most of them would not go. So Friso set fire to the village and all the royal storehouses; then no one could remain there, and all were glad to be out of it. We left everything behind us except wives and children, but we had an ample stock of provisions and warlike implements.

Friso was not yet satisfied. When we came to the old harbour, he went off with his stout soldiers and threw fire into all the ships that he could reach with his arrows. Six days later we saw the war-fleet of Demetrius coming down upon us. Friso ordered us to keep back the small ships in a broad line, and to put the large ships with the women and children in front. Further, he ordered us to take the crossbows that were in the fore part and fix them on the sterns of the ships, because, said he, we must fight a retreating battle. No man must presume to pursue a single enemy—that is my order. While we were busy about this, all at once the wind came ahead, to the great alarm of the cowards and the women, because we had no slaves except those who had voluntarily followed us. Therefore we could not escape the enemy by rowing. But Wr-alda knew well why he did this; and Friso, who understood it, immediately had the fire-arrows placed on the crossbows. At the same time he gave the order that no one should shoot before he did, and that we should all aim at the centre ship. If we succeeded in this, he said, the others would all go to its assistance, and then everybody might shoot as he best was able. When we were at a cable and a half distance from them the Phœnicians began to shoot, but Friso did not reply till the first arrow fell six fathoms from his ship. Then he fired, and the rest followed. It was like a shower of fire; and as our arrows went with the wind, they all remained alight and reached the third line. Everybody shouted and cheered, but the screams of our opponents were so loud that our hearts shrank. When Friso thought that it was sufficient he called us off, and we sped away; but after two days' slow sailing another fleet of thirty ships came in sight and gained upon us. Friso cleared for action again, but the others sent forward a small rowing-boat with messengers, who asked permission to sail with us, as they were Joniers. They had been compelled by Demetrius to go to the old haven; there they had heard of the battle, and girding on their stout swords, had followed us. Friso, who had sailed a good deal with the Joniers, said Yes; but Wichirte, our king, said No. The Joniers, said he, are worshippers of heathen gods; I myself have heard them call upon them. That comes from their intercourse with the real Greeks, Friso said. I have often done it myself, and yet I am as pious a Fryas man as any of you. Friso was the man to take us to Friesland, therefore the Joniers went with us. It seems that this was pleasing to Wr-alda, for before three months were past we coasted along Britain, and three days later we could shout huzza.

This Writing has been Given to Me about Northland and Schoonland (Scandinavia)

When our land was submerged I was in Schoonland. It was very bad there. There were great lakes which rose from the earth like bubbles, then burst asunder, and from the rents flowed a stuff like red-hot iron. The tops of high mountains fell and destroyed whole forests and villages. I myself saw one mountain torn from another and fall straight down. When I afterwards went to see the place there was a lake there. When the earth was composed there came a duke of Lindasburgt with his people, and one maiden who cried everywhere, Magy is the cause of all the misery that we have suffered. They continued their progress, and their hosts increased. The Magy fled, and his corpse was found where he had killed himself. Then the Finns were driven to one place where they might live. There were some of mixed blood who were allowed to stay, but most of them went with the Finns. The duke was chosen as king. The temples which had remained whole were destroyed. Since that time the good Northmen come often to Texland for the advice of the mother; still we cannot consider them real Frisians. In Denmark it has certainly happened as with us. The sea-people, who call themselves famous sea-warriors, went on board their ships, and afterwards went back again.

Hail!

Whenever the Carrier has completed a period, then posterity shall understand that the faults and misdeeds that the Brokmannen have brought with them belonged to their forefathers; therefore I will watch, and will describe as much of their manners as I have seen. The Geertmannen I can readily pass by. I have not had much to do with them, but as far as I have seen they have mostly retained their language and customs. I cannot say that of the others. Those who descend from the Greeks speak a bad language, and have not much to boast of in their manners. Many have brown eyes and hair. They are envious and impudent, and cowardly from superstition. When they speak, they put the words first that ought to come last. For old they at; for salt, sât; and for man, ma—too many to mention. They also use abbreviations of names, which have no meaning. The Joniers speak better, but they drop the H, and put it where it ought not to be. When they make a statue of a dead person they believe that the spirit of the departed enters into it; therefore they have hidden their statues of Frya, Fâsta, Medea, Thiania, Hellenia, and many others. When a child is born, all the relatives come together and pray to Frya to send her servants to bless the child. When they have prayed, they must neither move nor speak. If the child begins to cry, and continues some time, it is a bad sign, and they suspect that the mother has committed adultery. I have seen very bad things come from that. If the child sleeps, that is a good sign—Frya's servants are come. If it laughs in its sleep, the servants have promised it happiness. Moreover, they believe in bad spirits, witches, sorcerers, dwarfs, and elves, as if they descended from the Finns. Herewith I will finish, and I think I have written more than any of my forefathers. Frethorik.

Frethorik, my husband, lived to the age of 63. Since 108 years he is the first of his race who died a peaceable death; all the others died by violence, because they all fought with their own people, and with foreigners for right and duty.

My name is Wiljo. I am the maiden who came home with him from Saxsenmarken. In the course of conversation it came out that we were both of Adela's race—thus our affection commenced, and we became man and wife. He left me with five children, two sons and three daughters. Konreed was my eldest son, Hachgana my second. My eldest daughter is called Adela, my second Frulik, and the youngest Nocht. When I went to Saxsenmarken I preserved three books—the book of songs, the book of narratives, and the Hellenia book.

I write this in order that people may not think they were by Apollonia. I have had a good deal of annoyance about this, and therefore now wish to have the honour of it. I also did more. When Gosa Makonta died, whose goodness and clear-sightedness have become a proverb, I went alone to Texland to copy the writings that she had left; and when the last will of Frana was found, and the writings left by Adela or Hellenia, I did that again. These are the writings of Hellenia. I have put them first because they are the oldest.

Hail to all true Frisians.

In the olden times, the Slavonic race knew nothing of liberty. They were brought under the yoke like oxen. They were driven into the bowels of the earth to dig metals, and had to build houses of stone as dwelling-places for princes and priests. Of all that they did nothing came to themselves, everything must serve to enrich and make more powerful the priests and the princes, and to satisfy them. Under this treatment they grew gray and old before their time, and died without any enjoyment; although the earth produces abundantly for the good of all her children. But our runaways and exiles came through Twiskland to their boundaries, and our sailors came to their harbours. From them they heard of liberty, of justice, and laws, without which men cannot exist. This was all absorbed by the unhappy people like dew into an arid soil. When they fully understood this, the most courageous among them began to clank their chains, which grieved the princes. The princes are proud and warlike; there is therefore some virtue in their hearts. They consulted together and bestowed some of their superfluity; but the cowardly hypocritical priests could not suffer this. Among their false gods they had invented also wicked cruel monsters. Pestilence broke out in the country; and they said that the gods were angry with the domineering of the wicked. Then the boldest of the people were strangled in their chains. The earth drank their blood, and that blood produced corn and fruits that inspired with wisdom those who ate them.

Sixteen hundred years ago (she writes, 593 B.C.), Atland was submerged; and at that time something happened which nobody had reckoned upon. In the heart of Findasland, upon a mountain, lies a plain called Kasamyr

(Cashmere) that is "extraordinary." There was a child born whose mother was the daughter of a king, and whose father was a high-priest. In order to hide the shame they were obliged to renounce their own blood. Therefore it was taken out of the town to poor people. As the boy grew up, nothing was concealed from him, so he did all in his power to acquire wisdom. His intellect was so great that he understood everything that he saw or heard. The people regarded him with respect, and the priests were afraid of his questions. When he was of full age he went to his parents. They had to listen to some hard language; and to get rid of him they gave him a quantity of jewels, but they dared not openly acknowledge him. Overcome with sorrow at the false shame of his parents, he wandered about. While travelling he fell in with a Frisian sailor who was serving as a slave, and who taught him our manners and customs. He bought the freedom of the slave, and they remained friends till death. Wherever he went he taught the people not to tolerate rich men or priests, and that they must guard themselves against false shame, which everywhere did harm to love and charity. The earth, he said, bestowed her treasures on those who scratch her skin; so all are obliged to dig, and plough, and sow if they wish to reap, but no one is obliged to do anything for another unless it be out of goodwill. He taught that men should not seek in her bowels for gold, or silver, or precious stones, which occasion envy and destroy love. To embellish your wives and daughters, he said, the river offers her pure stream. No man is able to make everybody equally rich and happy, but it is the duty of all men to make each other as equally rich and as happy as possible. Men should not despise any knowledge; but justice is the greatest knowledge that time can teach, because she wards off offences and promotes love.

His first name was Jessos, but the priests, who hated him, called him Fo, that is, false; the people called him Krishna, that is, shepherd; and his Frisian friend called him Buddha (purse), because he had in his head a treasure of wisdom, and in his heart a treasure of love.

At last he was obliged to flee from the wrath of the priests; but wherever he went his teaching had preceded him, whilst his enemies followed him like his shadow. When Jessos had thus travelled for twelve years he died; but his friends preserved his teaching, and spread it wherever they found listeners.

What do you think the priests did then? That I must tell you, and you must give your best attention to it. Moreover, you must keep guard against their acts and their tricks with all the strength that Wr-alda has given you. While the doctrine of Jessos was thus spreading over the earth, the false priests went to the land of his birth to make his death known. They said they were his friends, and they pretended to show great sorrow by tearing their clothes and shaving their heads. They went to live in caves in the mountains, but in them they had hid all their treasures, and they made in them images of Jessos. They gave these statues to simple people, and at last they said that Jessos was a god, that he had declared this himself to them, and that all those who followed his doctrine should enter his kingdom hereafter, where all was joy and happiness. Because they knew that he was opposed to the rich, they announced everywhere that poverty, suffering, and humility were the door by which to enter into his kingdom, and that those who had suffered the most on earth should enjoy the greatest happiness there. Although they knew that Jessos had taught that men should regulate and control their passions, they taught that men should stifle their passions, and that the perfection of humanity consisted in being as unfeeling as the cold stones. In order to make the people believe that they did as they preached, they pretended to outward poverty; and that they had overcome all sensual feelings, they took no wives. But if any young girl had made a false step, it was quickly forgiven; the weak, they said, were to be assisted, and to save their souls men must give largely to the Church. Acting in this way, they had wives and children without households, and were rich without working; but the people grew poorer and more miserable than they had ever been before. This doctrine, which requires the priests to possess no further knowledge than to speak deceitfully, and to pretend to be pious while acting unjustly, spreads from east to west, and will come to our land also.

But when the priests fancy that they have entirely extinguished the light of Frya and Jessos, then shall all classes of men rise up who have quietly preserved the truth among themselves, and have hidden it from the priests. They shall be of princely blood of priests, Slavonic, and Frya's blood. They will make their light visible, so that all men shall see the truth; they shall cry woe to the acts of the princes and the priests. The princes who love the truth and justice shall separate themselves from the priests; blood shall flow, but from it the people will gather new strength. Finda's folk shall contribute their industry to the common good, Linda's folk their strength, and we our wisdom. Then the false priests shall be swept away from the earth. Wr-alda's spirit shall be invoked everywhere and always; the laws that Wr-alda in the beginning instilled into our consciences shall alone be listened to. There shall be neither princes, nor masters, nor rulers, except those chosen by the general voice. Then Frya shall rejoice, and the earth will only bestow her gifts on those who work. All this shall begin 4000 years after the submersion of Atland, and 1000 years later there shall exist no longer either priest or oppression.

Dela, surnamed Hellenia, watch!

Thus runs Frana's last will: All noble Frisians, Heil! In the name of Wralda, of Frya, and of Freedom, I greet you; and pray you if I die before I have named a successor, then I recommend to you Teuntja, who is Burgtmaagd in the citadel of Medeasblik; till now she is the best.

This Gosa has left behind her: Hail to all men! I have named no Eeremoeder, because I know none, and because it is better for you to have no mother than to have one you cannot trust. One bad time is passed by, but there is still another coming. Irtha has not given it birth, and Wr-alda has not decreed it. It comes from the East, out of the bosom of the priests. It will breed so much mischief that Irtha will not be able to drink the blood of her slain children. It will spread darkness over the minds of men like storm-clouds over the sunlight. Everywhere craft and deception shall contend with freedom and justice. Freedom and justice shall be overcome, and we with them. But this success will work out its own loss. Our descendants shall teach their people and their slaves the meaning of three words; they are universal love, freedom, and justice. At first they shall shine, then struggle with darkness, until every man's head and heart has become bright and clear. Then shall oppression be driven from the earth, like the thunder-clouds by the storm-wind, and all deceit will cease to have any more power. Gosa.

The Writing of Konerêd

My forefathers have written this book in succession. I will do this, the more because there exists no longer in my state any citadel on which events are inscribed as used to be the case. My name is Konerêd (Koenraad). My father's name was Frethorik, my mother's name was Wiljow. After my father's death I was chosen as his successor. When I was fifty years old I was chosen for chief Grevetman. My father has written how the Lindaoorden and Liudgaarden were destroyed. Lindahem is still lost, the Lindaoorden partially, and the north Lindgaarden are still concealed by the salt sea. The foaming sea washes the ramparts of the castle. As my father has mentioned, the people, being deprived of their harbour, went away and built houses inside the ramparts of the citadel; therefore that bastion is called Lindwerd. The sea-people say Linwerd, but that is nonsense. In my youth there was a portion of land lying outside the rampart all mud and marsh; but Frya's people were neither tired nor exhausted when they had a good object in view. By digging ditches, and making dams of the earth that came out of the ditches, we recovered a good space of land outside the rampart, which had the form of a hoof three poles eastward, three southwards, and three westwards. At present we are engaged in ramming piles into the ground to make a harbour to protect our rampart. When the work is finished we shall attract mariners. In my youth it looked very queer, but now there stands a row of houses. Leaks and deficiencies produced by poverty have been remedied by industry. From this men may learn that Wr-alda, our universal father, protects all his creatures, if they preserve their courage and help each other.

Now I Will Write about Friso

Friso, who was already powerful by his troops, was chosen chief Grevetman of the districts round Staveren. He laughed at our mode of defending our land and our sea-fights; therefore he established a school where the boys might learn to fight in the Greek manner, but I believe that he did it to attach the young people to himself. I sent my brother there ten years ago, because I thought, now that we have not got any mother, it behoves me to be doubly watchful, in order that he may not become our master.

Gosa has given us no successors. I will not give any opinion about that; but there are still old suspicious people who think that she and Friso had an understanding about it. When Gosa died, the people from all parts wished to choose another mother; but Friso, who was busy establishing a kingdom for himself, did not desire to have any advice or messenger from Texland. When the messengers of the Landsaten came to him, he said that Gosa had been far-seeing and wiser than all the counts together, and yet she had been unable to see any light or way out of this affair; therefore she had not had the courage to choose a successor, and to choose a doubtful one she thought would be very bad; therefore she wrote in her last will, It is better to have no mother than to have one on whom you cannot rely. Friso had seen a great deal. He had been brought up in the wars, and he had just learned and gathered as much of the tricks and cunning ways of the Gauls and the princes as he required, to lead the other counts wherever he wished. See here how he went to work about that.

Friso had taken here another wife, a daughter of Wilfrêthe, who in his lifetime had been chief count of Staveren. By her he had two sons and two daughters. By his wish Kornelia, his youngest daughter, was married to my brother. Kornelia is not good Frisian; her name ought to be written Kornhelia. Weemoed, his eldest daughter, he married to Kauch. Kauch, who went to school to him, is the son of Wichhirte, the king of the Geertmen. But Kauch is likewise not good Frisian, and ought to be Kaap (Koop). So they have learned more bad language than good manners.

Now I must return to my story.

After the great flood of which my father wrote an account, there came many Jutlanders and Letlanders out of the Baltic, or bad sea. They were driven down the Kattegat in their boats by the ice as far as the coast of Denmark, and there they remained. There was not a creature to be seen; so they took possession of the land, and named it after themselves, Jutland. Afterwards many of the Denmarkers returned from the higher lands, but they settled more to the south; and when the mariners returned who had not been lost, they all went together to Zeeland. By this arrangement the

Jutlanders retained the land to which Wr-alda had conducted them. The Zeeland skippers, who were not satisfied to live upon fish, and who hated the Gauls, took to robbing the Phœnician ships. In the south-west point of Scandinavia there lies Lindasburgt, called Lindasnôse, built by one Apol, as is written in the book. All the people who live on the coasts, and in the neighbouring districts, had remained true Frisians; but by their desire for vengeance upon the Gauls, and the followers of Kaltona, they joined the Zeelanders. But that connection did not hold together, because the Zeelanders had adopted many evil manners and customs of the wicked Magyars, in opposition to Frya's people. Afterwards, everybody went stealing on his own account; but when it suited them they held all together. At last the Zeelanders began to be in want of good ships. Their shipbuilders had died, and their forests as well as their land had been washed out to sea. Now there arrived unexpectedly three ships, which anchored off the ringdyk of our citadel. By the disruption of our land they had lost themselves, and had missed Flymond. The merchant who was with them wished to buy new ships from us, and for that purpose had brought all kinds of valuables, which they had stolen from the Celtic country and Phœnician ships. As we had no ships, I gave them active horses and four armed couriers to Friso; because at Stavere, along the Alberga, the best ships of war were built of hard oak which never rots. While these sea rovers remained with us, some of the Jutmen had gone to Texland, and thence to Friso. The Zeelanders had stolen many of their strongest boys to row their ships, and many of their finest daughters to have children by. The great Jutlanders could not prevent it, as they were not properly armed. When they had related all their misfortunes, and a good deal of conversation had taken place, Friso asked them at last if they had no good harbours in their country. Oh, yes, they answered; a beautiful one, created by Wr-alda. It is like a bottle, the neck narrow, but in the belly a thousand large boats may lie; but we have no citadel and no defences to keep out the pirate ships. Then you should make them, said Friso. That is very good advice, said the Jutlanders; but we have no workmen and no building materials; we are all fishermen and trawlers. The others are drowned or fled to the higher lands. While they were talking in this way, my messengers arrived at the court with the Zeeland gentlemen. Here you must observe how Friso understood deceiving everybody, to the satisfaction of both parties, and to the accomplishment of his own ends. To the Zeelanders he promised that they should have yearly fifty ships of a fixed size for a fixed price, fitted with iron chains and crossbows, and full rigging as is necessary and useful for men-of-war, but that they should leave in peace the Jutlanders and all the people of Frya's race. But he wished to do more; he wanted to engage all our sea rovers to go with him upon his fighting expedition. When the Zeelanders had gone, he loaded forty old ships with weapons for wall defences, wood, bricks, carpenters, masons, and smiths, in order to build citadels. Witto, or Witte, his son, he sent to superintend. I have never been well informed of what happened; but this much is clear to me, that on each side of the harbour a strong citadel has been built, and garrisoned by people brought by Friso out of Saksenmarken. Witto courted Siuchthirte and married her. Wilhem, her father, was chief Alderman of the Jutmen—that is, chief Grevetman or Count. Wilhem died shortly afterwards, and Witto was chosen in his place.

What Friso did Further

Of his first wife he still had two brothers-in-law, who were very daring. Hetto—that is, heat—the youngest, he sent as messenger to Kattaburgt, which lies far in the Saxsenmarken. Friso gave him to take seven horses, besides his own, laden with precious things stolen by the sea-rovers. With each horse there were two young sea-rovers and two young horsemen, clad in rich garments, and with money in their purses. In the same way as he sent Hetto to Kattaburgt, he sent Bruno—that is, brown—the other brother-in-law, to Mannagarda oord, Mannagarda oord was written Mannagarda ford in the earlier part of this book, but that is wrong. All the riches that they took with them were given away, according to circumstances, to princes, princesses, and chosen young girls. When his young men went to the tavern to dance with the young people there, they ordered baskets of spice, gingerbread, and tuns of the best beer. After these messengers he let his young people constantly go over to the Saxsenmarken, always with money in their purses and presents to give away, and they spent money carelessly in the taverns. When the Saxsen youths looked with envy at this they smiled, and said, If you dare go and fight the common enemy you would be able to give much richer presents to your brides, and live much more princely. Both the brothers-in-law of Friso had married daughters of the chief princes, and afterwards the Saxsen youths and girls came in whole troops to the Flymeer.

The burgtmaidens and old maidens who still remembered their greatness did not hold with Friso's object, and therefore they said no good of him; but Friso, more cunning than they, let them chatter, but the younger maidens he led to his side with golden fingers. They said everywhere, For a long time we have had no mother, but that comes from our being fit to take care of ourselves. At present it suits us best to have a king to win back our lands that we have lost through the imprudence of our mothers. Further they said, Every child of Frya has permission to let his voice be heard before the choice of a prince is decided; but if it comes to that, that you choose a king, then also we will have our say. From all that we can see, Wr-alda has appointed Friso for it, for he has brought him here in a wonderful way. Friso knows the tricks of the Gauls, whose language he speaks; he can therefore watch against their craftiness. Then there is something else to keep the eye upon. What count could be chosen as king without the others being jealous of him? All such nonsense the young maidens talked; but the old maidens, though few in number, tapped their advice out of another cask. They said always and to every one: Friso does like the spiders. At night he spreads his webs in all directions, and in the day he catches in them all his unsuspecting friends. Friso says he cannot suffer any priests or foreign princes, but we say that he cannot suffer anybody but himself; therefore he will not allow the citadel of Stavia to be rebuilt; therefore he will not have the mother again. To-day Friso is your counsellor, to-morrow he will be your king, in order to have full power over you. Among the people there now existed two parties. The old and the poor wished to have the mother again, but the young and the warlike wished for a father and a king. The first called themselves mother's sons, the others father's sons, but the mother's sons did not count for much; because there were many ships to build, there was a good time for all kinds of workmen. Moreover, the sea-rovers brought all sorts of treasures, with which the maidens were pleased, the girls were pleased, and their relations and friends.

When Friso had been nearly forty years at Staveren he died. Owing to him many of the states had been joined together again, but that we were the better for it I am not prepared to certify. Of all the counts that preceded him there was none so renowned as Friso; for, as I said before, the young maidens spoke in his praise, while the old maidens did all in their power to make him hateful to everybody. Although the old women could not prevent his meddling, they made so much fuss that he died without becoming king.

Now I will Write about His Son Adel

Friso, who had learned our history from the book of the Adelingen, had done everything in his power to win their friendship. His eldest son, whom he had by his wife Swethirte, he named Adel; and although he strove with all his might to prevent the building or restoring any citadels, he sent Adel to the citadel of Texland in order to make himself better acquainted with our laws, language, and customs. When Adel was twenty years old Friso brought him into his own school, and when he had fully educated him he sent him to travel through all the states. Adel was an amiable young man, and in his travels he made many friends, so the people called him Atharik— that is, rich in friends—which was very useful to him afterwards, for when his father died he took his place without a question of any other count being chosen.

While Adel was studying at Texland there was a lovely maiden at the citadel. She came from Saxenmarken, from the state of Suobaland, therefore she was called at Texland Suobene, although her name was Ifkja. Adel fell in love with her, and she with him, but his father wished him to wait a little. Adel did as he wished; but as soon as he was dead, sent messengers to Berthold, her father, to ask her in marriage. Berthold was a prince of high-principled feelings. He had sent his daughter to Texland in the hope that she might be chosen Burgtmaagd in her country, but when he knew of their mutual affection he bestowed his blessing upon them. Ifkja was a clever Frisian. As far as I have been able to learn, she always toiled and worked to bring the Frya's people back under the same laws and customs. To bring the people to her side, she travelled with her husband through all Saxenmarken, and also to Geertmannia—as the Geertmen had named the country which they had obtained by means of Gosa. Thence they went to Denmark, and from Denmark by sea to Texland. From Texland they went to Westflyland, and so along the coast to Walhallagara; thence they followed the Zuiderryn (the Waal), till, with great apprehension, they arrived beyond the Rhine at the Marsaten of whom our Apollonia has written. When they had stayed there a little time, they returned to the lowlands. When they had been some time descending towards the lowlands, and had reached about the old citadel of Aken, four of their servants were suddenly murdered and stripped. They had loitered a little behind. My brother, who was always on the alert, had forbidden them to do so, but they did not listen to him. The murderers that had committed this crime were Twisklanders, who had at that time audaciously crossed the Rhine to murder and to steal. The Twisklanders are banished and fugitive children of Frya, but their wives they have stolen from the Tartars. The Tartars are a brown tribe of Finda's people, who are thus named because they make war on everybody. They are all horsemen and robbers. This is what makes the Twisklanders so bloodthirsty. The Twisklanders who had done the wicked deed called themselves Frijen or Franken. There were among them, my brother said, red, brown, and white men. The red and brown made their hair white with lime-water—but as their faces remained brown, they were only the more ugly. In the same way as Apollonia, they visited Lydasburgt and the Aldergage. Afterwards they made a tour of all the neighbourhood of Stavera. They behaved with so much amiability, that everywhere the people wished to keep them. Three months later, Adel sent messengers to all the friends that he had made, requesting them to send to him their "wise men" in the month of May.

his wife, he said, who had been maagd of Texland, had received a copy of it. In Texland many writings are still found which are not copied in the book of the Adelingen. One of these writings had been placed by Gosa with her last will, which was to be opened by the oldest maiden, Albetha, as soon as Friso was dead.

Here is the Writing with Gosa's Advice

When Wr-alda gave children to the mothers of mankind, he gave one language to every tongue and to all lips. This gift Wr-alda had bestowed upon men in order that by its means they might make known to each other what must be avoided and what must be followed to find salvation, and to hold salvation to all eternity. Wr-alda is wise and good, and all-foreseeing. As he knew that happiness and holiness would flee from the earth when wickedness could overcome virtue, he has attached to the language an equitable property. This property consists in this, that men can neither lie nor use deceitful words without stammering or blushing, by which means the innately bad are easily known.

As thus our language opens the way to happiness and blessedness, and thus helps to guard against evil inclinations, it is rightly named the language of the gods, and all those by whom it is held in honour derive honour from it. But what has happened? As soon as among our half brothers and sisters deceivers arose, who gave themselves out as servants of the good, it soon became otherwise. The deceitful priests and the malignant princes, who always clung together, wished to live according to their own inclinations, without regard to the laws of right. In their wickedness they went so far as to invent other languages, so that they might speak secretly in anybody's presence of their wicked and unworthy affairs without betraying themselves by stammering, and without showing a blush upon their countenances. But what has that produced? Just as the seed of good herbs which has been sown by good men in the open day springs up from the ground, so time brings to light the evil seed which has been sown by wicked men in secret and in darkness.

The wanton girls and effeminate youths who consorted with the immoral priests and princes, taught the new language to their companions, and thus spread it among the people till God's language was clean forgotten. Would you know what came of all this? how that stammering and blushing no longer betrayed their evil doings;—virtue passed away, wisdom and liberty followed; unity was lost, and quarrelling took its place; love flew away, and unchastity and envy met round their tables; and where previously justice reigned, now it is the sword. All are slaves—the subjects of their masters, envy, bad passions and covetousness. If they had only invented one language things might possibly have still gone on well; but they invented as many languages as there are states, so that one people can no more understand another people than a cow a dog, or a wolf a sheep. The mariners can bear witness to this. From all this it results that all the slave people look upon each other as strangers; and that as a punishment of their inconsiderateness and presumption, they must quarrel and fight till they are all destroyed.

Here is my Counsel

If you wish that you alone should inherit the earth, you must never allow any language but God's language to pass your lips, and take care that your own language remains free from outlandish sounds. If you wish that some of Lyda's children and some of Finda's children remain, you must do the same. The language of the East Schoonlanders has been perverted by the vile Magyars, and the language of the followers of Kaltana has been spoiled by the dirty Gauls. Now, we have been weak enough to admit among us the returned followers of Hellenia, but I anxiously fear that they will reward our weakness by debasing our pure language.

Many things have happened to us, but among all the citadels that have been disturbed and destroyed in the bad time, Irtha has preserved Fryasburgt uninjured; and I may remark that Frya's or God's language has always remained here untainted.

Here in Texland, therefore, schools should be established; and from all the states that have kept to the old customs the young people should be sent here, and afterwards those whose education is complete can help those who remain at home. If foreigners come to buy ironwares from you, and want to talk and bargain, they must come back to God's language. If they learn God's language, then the words, "to be free" and "to have justice," will come to them, and glimmer and glitter in their brains to a perfect light, and that flame will destroy all bad princes and hypocritical dirty priests.

The native and foreign messengers were pleased with that writing, but no schools came from it. Then Adel established schools himself. Every year Adel and Ifkja went to inspect the schools. If they found a friendly feeling existing between the natives and foreigners, they were extremely pleased. If there were any who had sworn friendship together, they assembled the people, and with great ceremony let them inscribe their names in a book which was called the Book of Friendship, and afterwards a festival was held. All these customs were kept up in order to bring together the separate branches of Frya's race; but the maidens who were opposed to Adel and Ifkja said that they did it for no other reason than to make a name for themselves, and to bring all the other states under their subjection.

Among my father's papers I found a letter from Liudgert the Geertman. Omitting some passages which only concern my father, I proceed to relate the rest.

Punjab, that is five rivers, and by which we travel, is a river of extraordinary beauty, and is called Five Rivers, because four other streams flow into the sea by its mouth. Far away to the eastward is another large river, the Holy or Sacred Ganges. Between these two rivers is the land of the Hindoos. Both rivers run from the high mountains to the plains. The mountains in which their sources lie are so high that they reach the heavens (laia), and therefore these mountains are called Himmellaia. Among the Hindoos and others out of these countries there are people who meet together secretly. They believe that they are pure children of Finda, and that Finda was born in the Himmellaia mountains, whence she went with her children to the lowlands. Some of them believe that she, with her children, floated down upon the foam of the Ganges, and that that is the reason why the river is called the Sacred Ganges. But the priests, who came from another country, traced out these people and had them burnt, so that they do not dare to declare openly their creed. In this country all the priests are fat and rich. In their churches there are all kinds of monstrous images, many of them of gold. To the west of the Punjab are the Yren (Iraniers), or morose (Drangianen), the Gedrosten (Gedrosiers), or runaways, and the Urgetten, or forgotten. These names are given by the priests out of spite, because they fled from their customs and religion. On their arrival our forefathers likewise established themselves to the east of the Punjab, but on account of the priests they likewise went to the west. In that way we learned to know the Yren and other people. The Yren are not savages, but good people, who neither pray to nor tolerate images; neither will they suffer priests or churches; but as we adhere to the light of Fasta, so they everywhere maintain fire in their houses. Coming still further westward, we arrive at the Gedrosten. Regarding the Gedrosten: They have been mixed with other people, and speak a variety of languages. These people are really savage murderers, who always wander about the country on horseback hunting and robbing, and hire themselves as soldiers to the surrounding princes, at whose command they destroy whatever they can reach.

 The country between the Punjab and the Ganges is as flat as Friesland near the sea, and consists of forests and fields, fertile in every part, but this does not prevent the people from dying by thousands of hunger. The famines, however, must not be attributed to Wr-alda or Irtha, but to the princes and priests. The Hindoos are timid and submissive before their princes, like hinds before wolves. Therefore the Yren and others have called them Hindoos, which means hinds. But their timidity is frightfully abused. If strangers come to purchase corn, everything is turned into money, and this is not prevented by the priests, because they, being more crafty and rapacious than all the princes put together, know very well that all the money will come into their pockets. Besides what the people suffer from their princes, they suffer a great deal from poisonous and wild beasts. There are great elephants that sometimes go about in whole flocks and trample down corn-fields and whole villages. There are great black and white cats which are called tigers. They are as large as calves, and they devour both men and beasts. Besides other creeping animals there are snakes from the size of a worm to the size of a tree. The largest can swallow a cow, but the smallest are the most deadly. They conceal themselves among the fruits and flowers, and surprise the people who come to gather them. Any one who is bitten by them is sure to die, as Irtha has given no antidote to their poison, because the people have so given themselves up to idolatry. There are, besides, all sorts of lizards, tortoises, and crocodiles. All these reptiles, like the snakes, vary from the size of a worm to the trunk of a tree. According to their size and fierceness, they have names which I cannot recollect, but the largest are called alligators, because they eat as greedily the putrid cattle that float down the stream as they do living animals that they seize. On the west of the Punjab where we come from, and where I was born, the same fruits and crops grow as on the east side. Formerly there existed also the same crawling animals, but our forefathers burnt all the underwood, and so diligently hunted all the wild animals, that there are scarcely any left. To the extreme west of the Punjab there is found rich clay land as well as barren heaths, which seem endless, occasionally varied lovely spots on which the eye rests enchanted. Among the fruits there are many that I have not found here. Among the various kinds of corn some is as yellow as gold. There are also golden apples, of which some are as sweet as honey and others as sour as vinegar. In our country there are nuts as large as a child's head. They contain cheese and milk. When they are old oil is made from them. Of the husks ropes are made, and of the shells cups and other household utensils are made. I have found in the woods here bramble and holly berries. In my country we have trees bearing berries, as large as your lime-trees, the berries of which are much sweeter and three times as large as your gooseberries. When the days are at the longest, and the sun is in the zenith, a man's body has no shadow. If you sail very far to the south and look to the east at midday, the sun shines on your left side as it does in other countries on the right side. With this I will finish. It will be easy for you, by means of what I have written, to distinguish between false accounts and true descriptions.— Your Luidgert.

The Writing of Beeden

My name is Beeden, son of Hachgana. My uncle, not having married, left no children. I was elected in his place. Adel, the third king of that name, approved of the choice, provided I should acknowledge him as master. In addition to the entire inheritance of my uncle, he gave me some land which joined my inheritance, on condition that I would settle people there who should never his people…therefore I will allow it a place here.

Letter of Rika the Oudmaagd, Read at Staveren at the Juul Feast

My greeting to all of you whose forefathers came here with Friso. According to what you say, you are not guilty of idolatry. I will not speak about that now, but will at once mention a failing which is very little better. You know, or you do not know, how many titles Wr-alda has; but you all know that he is named universal provider, because that everything comes and proceeds from him for the sustenance of his creatures. It is true that Irtha is named sometimes the feeder of all, because she brings forth all the fruits and grains on which men and beasts are fed; but she would not bear any fruit or grain unless Wr-alda gave her the power. Women who nourish their children at their breasts are called nurses, but if Wr-alda did not give them milk the children would find no advantage; so that, in short, Wr-alda really is the nourisher. That Irtha should be called the universal nourisher, and that a mother should be called a feeder, one can understand, figuratively speaking; but that a father should be called a feeder, because he is a father, goes against all reason. Now I know whence all this folly comes. Listen to me. It comes from our enemies; and if this is followed up you will become slaves, to the sorrow of Frya and to the punishment of your pride, I will tell you what happened to the slave people; from that you may take warning. The foreign kings, who follow their own will, place Wr-alda below the crown. From envy that Wr-alda is called the universal father, they wish also to be called fathers of the people. Now, everybody knows that kings do not regulate the productiveness of the earth; and that they have their sustenance by means of the people, but still they will persist in their arrogance. In order to attain their object they were not satisfied from the beginning with free gifts, but imposed a tax upon the people. With the tax thus raised they hired foreign soldiers, whom they retained about their courts. Afterwards they took as many wives as they pleased, and the smaller princes and gentry did the same. When, in consequence, quarrels and disputes arose in the households, and complaints were made about it, they said every man is the father (feeder) of his household, therefore he shall be master and judge over it. Thus arose arbitrariness, and as the men ruled over their households the kings would do over their people. When the kings had accomplished that, they should be called fathers of the people, they had statues of themselves made, and erected in the churches beside the statues of the idols, and those who would not bow down to them were either killed or put in chains. Your forefathers and the Twisklanders had intercourse with the kings, and learned these follies from them. But it is not only that some of your men have been guilty of stealing titles, I have also much to complain of against your wives. If there are men among you who wish to put themselves on a level with Wr-alda, there are also women who wish to consider themselves equals of Frya. Because they have borne children, they call themselves mothers; but they forget that Frya bore children without having intercourse with a man. Yes, they not only have desired to rob Frya and the Eeremoeders of their honourable title (with whom they cannot put themselves upon an equality), but they do the same with the honourable titles of their fellow-creatures. There are women who allow themselves to be called ladies, although they know that that only belongs to the wives of princes. They also let their daughters be called maagden, although they know that no young girls are so called unless they belong to a citadel. You all fancy that you are the better for this name-stealing, but you forget that jealousy clings to it, and that every wrong sows the seed of its own rod. If you do not alter your course, in time it will grow so strong that you cannot see what will be the end. Your descendants will be flogged by it, and will not know whence the stripes come. But although you do not build citadels for the maidens and leave them to their fate, there will still remain some who will come out of woods and caves, and will prove to your descendants that you have by your disorderliness been the cause of it. Then you will be damned. Your ghosts will rise frightened out of their graves. They will call upon Wr-alda, Frya, and her maidens, but they shall receive no succour before the Juul shall enter upon a new circuit, and that will only be three thousand years after this century.

The end of Rika's letter...therefore I will first write about black Adel. Black Adel was the fourth king after Friso. In his youth he studied first at Texland, and then at Staveren, and afterwards travelled through all the states. When he was twenty-four years old his father had him elected Asega-Asker. As soon as he became Asker he always took the part of the poor. The rich, he said, do enough of wrong by means of their wealth, therefore we ought to take care that the poor look up to us. By arguments of this kind he became the friend of the poor and the terror of the rich. It was carried so far that his father looked up to him. When his father died he succeeded, and then he wished to retain his office as well, as the kings of the East used to do. The rich would not suffer this, so all the people rose up, and the rich were glad to get out of the assembly with whole skins. From that time there was no more talk of equality. He oppressed the rich and flattered the poor, by whose assistance he succeeded in all his wishes. King Askar, as he was always called, was seven feet high, and his strength was as remarkable as his height. He had a clear intellect, so that he understood all that was talked about, but in his actions he did not display much wisdom. He had a handsome countenance and a smooth tongue, but his soul was blacker than his hair. When he had been king for a year, he obliged all the young men in the state to come once a year to the camp to have a sham fight. At first he had some trouble with it, but at last it became such a habit that old and young came from all sides to ask if they might take part in it. When he had brought it to this point, he established military schools. The rich complained that their children no longer learned to read and write. Askar paid no attention to it; but shortly afterwards, when a sham fight was held, he mounted a throne and spoke aloud: The rich have come to complain to me that their boys do not learn to read and write. I answered nothing; but I will now declare my opinion, and let the general assembly decide. While they all regarded him with curiosity, he said further: According to my idea, we ought to leave reading and writing at present to the maagden and wise people. I do not wish to speak ill of our forefathers; I will only say that in the times so vaunted by some, the Burgtmaagden introduced disputes into our country, which the mothers were unable, either first or last, to put an end to. Worse still, while they talked and chattered about useless customs the Gauls came and seized all our beautiful southern country. Even at this very time our degenerate brothers and their soldiers have already come over the Scheldt. It therefore remains for us to choose whether we will carry a yoke or a sword. If we wish to be and to remain free, it behoves our young men to leave reading and writing alone for a time; and instead of playing games of swinging and wrestling, they must learn to play with sword and spear. When we are completely prepared, and the boys are big enough to carry helmet and shield and to use their weapons, then, with your help, I will attack the enemy. The Gauls may then record the defeat of their helpers and soldiers upon our fields with the blood that flows from their wounds. When we have once expelled the enemy, then we must follow it up till there are no more Gauls, Slaves, or Tartars to be driven out of Frya's inheritance. That is right, the majority shouted, and the rich did not dare to open their mouths.

He must certainly have thought over this address and had it written out, for on the evening of the same day there were copies in at least twenty different hands, and they all sounded the same. Afterwards he ordered the ship people to make double prows, upon which steel crossbows could be fixed. Those who were backward in doing this were fined, and if they swore that they had no means, the rich men of the village were obliged to pay. Now we shall see what resulted from all this bustle. In the north part of Britain there exists a Scotch people—the most of them spring from Frya's blood—some of them are descended from the followers of Keltana, and, for the rest, from Britons and fugitives who gradually, in the course of time, took refuge there from the tin mines. Those who come from the tin mines have wives, either altogether foreign or of foreign descent They are all under the dominion of the Gauls. Their arms are wooden bows and arrows pointed with stag's-horn or flint. Their houses are of turf and straw, and some of them live in caves in the mountains. Sheep that they have stolen form their only wealth. Some of the descendants of Keltana's followers still have iron weapons, which they have inherited from their forefathers. In order to make myself well understood, I must let alone for a while my account of the Scotch people, and write something about the near Krekalanders (Italians). The Krekalanders formerly belonged to us only, but from time immemorial descendants of Lyda and Finda have established themselves there. Of these last there came in the end a whole troop from Troy. Troy is the name of a town that the far Krekalanders (Greeks) had taken and destroyed. When the Trojans had nestled themselves among the near Krekalanders, with time and industry they built a strong town with walls and citadels named Rome, that is, Spacious. When this was done, the people by craft and force made themselves masters of the whole land. The people who live on the south side of the Mediterranean Sea, come for the most part from Phœnicia. The Phœnicians (Puniers or Carthaginians) are a bastard race of the blood of Frya, Finda, and Lyda. The Lyda people were there as slaves, but by the unchastity of the women these black people have degenerated the other people and dyed them brown. These people and the Romans are constantly struggling for the supremacy over the Mediterranean Sea. The Romans, moreover, live at enmity with the Phœnicians; and their priests, who wish to assume the sole government of the world, cannot bear the sight of the Gauls. First they took from the Phoenicians Marseilles—then all the countries lying to the south, the west, and the north, as well as the southern part of Britain—and they have always driven away the Phœnician priests, that is the Gauls, of whom thousands have sought refuge in North Britain. A short time ago the chief of the Gauls was established in the citadel, which is called Kerenac (Karnac), that is the corner, whence he issued his commands to the Gauls. All their gold was likewise collected there. Keeren Herne (chosen corner), or Kerenac, is a stone citadel which did belong to Kalta. Therefore the maidens of the descendants of Kaltana's followers wished to have the citadel again. Thus through the enmity of the maidens and the Gaul's, hatred and quarrelling spread ever the mountain country with fire and sword. Our sea people often came there to get wool, which they paid for with prepared hides and linen. Askar had often gone with them, and had secretly made friendship with the maidens and some princes, and bound himself to drive the Gauls out of Kerenac. When he came back there again he gave to the princes and the fighting men iron helmets and steel bows. War had come with him, and soon blood was streaming down the slopes of the mountains. When Askar thought a favourable opportunity occurred, he vent with forty ships and took Kerenac and the chief of the Gauls, with all his gold. The people with whom he fought against the soldiers of the Gauls, he had enticed out of the Saxenmarken by promises of much booty and plunder. Thus nothing was left to the Gauls. After that he took two islands for stations for his ships, from which he used later to sally forth and plunder all the Phœnician ships and towns that he could reach. When he returned he brought nearly six hundred of the finest youths of the Scotch mountaineers with him. He said that they had been given him as hostages, that he might be sure that the parents would remain faithful to him; but this was untrue. He kept them as a bodyguard at his court, where they had daily lessons in riding and in the use of all kinds of arms. The Denmarkers, who proudly considered themselves sea-warriors above all the other sea-people, no sooner heard of the glorious deeds of Askar, than they became jealous of him to such a degree, that they would bring war over the sea and over his lands. See here, then, how he was able to avoid a war. Among the ruins of the destroyed citadel of Stavia there was still established a clever Burgtmaagd, with a few maidens. Her name was Reintja, and she was famed for her wisdom. This maid offered her assistance to Askar, on condition that he should afterwards rebuild the citadel of Stavia. When he had bound himself to do this, Reintja went with three maidens to Hals (Holstein). She travelled by night, and by day she made speeches in all the markets and in all the assemblies. Wr-alda, she said, had told her by his thunder that all the Frya's people must become friends, and united as brothers and sisters, otherwise Finda's people would come and sweep them off the face of the earth. After the thunder Frya's seven watch-maidens appeared to her in a dream seven nights in succession. They had said, Disaster hovers over Frya's land with yoke and chains; therefore all the people who have sprung from Frya's blood must do away with their surnames, and only call themselves Frya's children, or Frya's people. They must all rise up and drive Finda's people out of Frya's inheritance. If you will not do that, you will bring the slave-chains round your necks, and the foreign chiefs will ill-treat your children and flog them till the blood streams into your graves. Then shall the spirits of your forefathers appear to you, and reproach your cowardice and thoughtlessness. The stupid people who, by the acts of the Magyars, were already so much accustomed to folly, believed all that she said, and the mothers clasped their children to their bosoms. When Reintja had brought the king of Holstein and the others to an agreement, she sent messengers to Askar, and went herself along the Baltic Sea. From there she went to the Lithauers (Face-hewers), so called because they always strike at their enemy's face. The Lithauers are fugitives and banished people of our own race, who wander about in the Twisklanden. Their wives have been mostly stolen from the Tartars. The Tartars are a branch of Finda's race, and are thus named by the Twisklanders because they never will be at peace, but provoke people to fight. She proceeded on beyond the Saxsenmarken, crossing through the other Twisklanders in order always to repeat the same thing. After two years had passed, she came along the Rhine home. Among the Twisklanders she gave herself out for a mother, and said that they might return as free and true people; but then they must go over the Rhine and drive the Gauls out of Frya's south lands. If they did that, then her King Askar would go over the Scheldt and win back the land. Among the Twisklanders many bad customs of the Tartars and Magyars have crept in, but likewise many of our laws have remained. Therefore they still have Maagden, who teach the children and advise the old. In the beginning they were opposed to Reintja, but at last she was followed, obeyed, and praised by them where it was useful or necessary.

As soon as Askar heard from Reintja's messengers how the Jutlanders were disposed, he immediately, on his side, sent messengers to the King of Hals. The ship in which the messengers went was laden with women's ornaments, and took also a golden shield on which Askar's portrait was artistically represented. These messengers were to ask the King's daughter, Frethogunsta, in marriage for Askar. Frethogunsta came a year after that to Staveren. Among her followers was a Magy, for the Jutlanders had been long ago corrupted. Soon after Askar had married Frethogunsta, a church was built at Staveren. In the church were placed monstrous images, bedecked with gold-woven dresses. It is also said that Askar, by night, and at unseasonable times, kneeled to them with Frethogunsta; but one thing is certain, the citadel of Stavia was never rebuilt. Reintja was already come back, and went angrily to Prontlik the mother, at Texland, to complain. Prontlik sent out messengers in all directions, who proclaimed that Askar is gone over to Idolatry. Askar took no notice of this, but unexpectedly a fleet arrived from Hals. In the night the maidens were driven out of the citadel, and in the morning there was nothing to be seen of the citadel but a glowing heap of rubbish. Prontlik and Reintja came to me for shelter. When I reflected upon it, I thought that it might prove bad for my state. Therefore, we hit upon a plan which might serve us all. This is the way we went to work. In the middle of the Krijlwood, to the east of Liudwerd, lies our place of refuge, which can only be reached by a concealed path. A long time ago I had established a garrison of young men who all hated Askar, and kept away all other people. Now it was come to such a pitch among us, that many women, and even men, talked about ghosts, white women, and gnomes, just like the Denmarkers. Askar had made use of all these follies for his own advantage, and we wished to do the same. One dark night I brought the Maagden to the citadel, and afterwards they went with their serving-maids dressed in white along the path, so that nobody dare go there any more. When Askar thought he had his hands free, he let the Magyars travel through his states under all kinds of names, and, except in my state, they were not turned away anywhere. After that Askar had become so connected with the Jutlanders and the Denmarkers, they all went roving together; but it produced no real good to them. They brought all sorts of foreign treasures home, and just for that reason the young men would learn no trades, nor work in the fields; so at last he was obliged to take slaves; but that was altogether contrary to Wr-alda's wish and to Frya's counsel. Therefore the punishment was sure to follow it. This is the way in which the punishment came. They had all together taken a whole fleet that came out of the Mediterranean Sea. This fleet was laden with purple cloths and other valuables that came from Phoenicia. The weak people of the fleet were put ashore south of the Seine, but the strong people were kept to serve as slaves. The handsomest were retained ashore, and the ugly and black were kept on board ship as rowers. In the Fly the plunder was divided, but, without their knowing it, they divided the punishment too. Of those who were placed in the foreign ships six died of colic. It was thought that the food and drink were poisoned, so it was all thrown overboard, but the colic remained all the same. Wherever the slaves or the goods came, there it came too. The Saxsenmen took it over to their marches. The Jutlanders brought it to Schoonland and along the coasts of the Baltic Sea, and with Askar's mariners it was taken to Britain. We and the people of Grênegâ did not allow either the people or the goods to come over our boundaries, and therefore we remained free from it. How many people were carried off by this disease I cannot tell; but Prontlik, who heard it afterwards from the maidens, told me that Askar had helped out of his states a thousand times more free-men than he had brought dirty slaves in. When the pest had ceased, the Twisklanders who had become free came to the Rhine, but Askar would not put himself on an equality with the princes of that vile degenerate race. He would not suffer them to call themselves Frya's children, as Reintja had offered them, but he forgot then that he himself had black hair. Among the Twisklanders there were two tribes who did not call themselves Twisklanders. One came from the far south-east, and called themselves Allemannen. They had given themselves this name when they had no women among them, and were wandering as exiles in the forests. Later on they stole women from the slave people like the Lithauers, but they kept their name. The other tribe, that wandered about in the neighbourhood, called themselves Franks, not because they were free, but the name of their first king was Frank, who, by the help of the degenerate maidens, had had himself made hereditary king over his people. The people nearest to him called themselves Thioth—his sons—that is, sons of the people. They had remained free, because they never would acknowledge any king, or prince, or master except those chosen by general consent in a general assembly. Askar had already learned from Reintja that the Twisklander princes were almost always at war with each other. He proposed to them that they should choose a duke from his people, because, as he said, he was afraid that they would quarrel among themselves for the supremacy. He said also that his princes could speak with the Gauls. This, he said, was also the opinion of the mother. Then the princes of the Twisklanders came together, and after twenty-one days they chose Alrik as duke. Alrik was Askar's nephew. He gave him two hundred Scotch and one hundred of the greatest Saksmannen to go with him as a bodyguard, The princes were to send twenty-one of their sons as hostages for their fidelity. Thus far all had gone according to his wishes; but when they were to go over the Rhine, the king of the Franks would not be under Alrik's command. Thereupon all was confusion. Askar, who thought that all was going on well, landed with his ships on the other side of the Scheldt; but there they were already aware of his coming, and were on their guard. He had to flee as quickly as he had come, and was himself taken prisoner. The Gauls did not know whom they had taken, so he was afterwards exchanged for a noble Gaul whom Askar's people had taken with them. While all this was going on, the Magyars went about audaciously over the lands of our neighbours. Near Egmuda, where formerly the citadel Forana had stood, they built a church larger and richer than that which Askar had built at Staveren. They said afterwards that Askar had lost the battle against the Gauls, because the people did not believe that Wodin could help them, and therefore they would not pray to him. They went about stealing young children, whom they kept and brought up in the mysteries of their abominable doctrines. Were there people who

(Here the manuscript ends abruptly...)

THE END

MARTINA MARTINE ANNOTATED CLASSICS
Check for more titles in our popular Annotated Classics series available exclusively on Amazon.com, including:

Lady Susan (Annotated) by Jane Austen
Androcles and the Lion (Annotated) by George Bernard Shaw
Agnes Grey (Annotated) by Anne Brontë
The Mysterious Affair at Styles (Annotated) by Agatha Christie

www.martinamartine.com

Manufactured by Amazon.ca
Acheson, AB